26.2

Julie Welch is a highly regarded sports writer, author and screenwriter. She has been a runner for four years and has run three London Marathons.

By the same author

FICTION

Dangerous Dancing

NON-FICTION

Long Distance Information
Leading Men
The World Cup: The Essential Guide to Mexico 86

26.2

Running the London Marathon

JULIE WELCH

YELLOW JERSEY PRESS
LONDON

Published by Yellow Jersey Press 2000

2 4 6 8 10 9 7 5 3 1

First published in Great Britain in 2000 by
Yellow Jersey Press
Random House, 20 Vauxhall Bridge Road,
London SW1V 2SA

Random House Australia (Pty) Limited
20 Alfred Street, Milsons Point, Sydney,
New South Wales 2061, Australia

Random House New Zealand Limited
18 Poland Road, Glenfield,
Auckland 10, New Zealand

Random House South Africa (Pty) Limited
Endulini, 5A Jubilee Road, Parktown 2193, South Africa

Random House UK Limited Reg. No. 954009

A CIP catalogue record for this book
is available from the British Library

ISBN 0 224 05982 3

Papers used by Random House UK Limited are natural,
recyclable products made from wood grown in sustainable forests;
the manufacturing processes conform to the environmental
regulations of the country of origin

Typeset by Deltatype Ltd, Birkenhead, Merseyside
Printed and bound in Great Britain by
Biddles Ltd, Guildford and King's Lynn

Dedicated to all the great people who make the London Marathon what it is – the runners themselves.

Photographic acknowledgements

Action Photos UK Ltd
Kevin Davies
Timothy Nunn
Ray O'Donoghue
Susie Rowbottham
Mark Shearman
Whizz-Kidz

Contents

Introduction

Every December I go a bit crazy and imagine myself speeding along the Embankment in the midday sun. I am lean but strong. My footsteps are as light as falling leaves and despite the toll of the last 25 miles my heartbeat is slow and steady. Only half a mile to go. Coming up Birdcage Walk the grass seems almost neon green after the grey hours of tarmac and blurred buildings. The crowd cheers and parts to let me through. I turn the corner into The Mall and it's there, the clock with its row of yellow digits, the last one blinking rhythmically, implacably – 3.59.56 . . . 57 . . . 58 . . . and I'm over the line. 3.59.59. Sub-four. *Yesss!*

I've got my entry for the London Marathon again.

Twenty-six point two miles in nearly four hours is a pretty modest time, to be honest. But you should see how long it took me last April. Abel Anton or Catherina MacKiernan could have gone round twice, and then some. I have short legs. My knees turn in. For the first 20 years of my adult life I smoked 40 cigarettes a day and stayed up half the night in bars drinking large amounts of vodka and snogging sports writers. My sole athletic triumph was in the Obstacle Race, Braeside Preparatory School, July 1957 (and if ever you catch me smiling in a quiet and private moment, the chances are I'm reliving it again: the flying start with both feet in a sack, the burning off of the opposition in the egg-and-spoon leg, the contemptuous ease with which I floated to the finish, bean bag on head).

The fact is that I've lived on this planet 50 years and where running is concerned I am quite awesomely untalented. But it doesn't matter a damn because late in life I found my vocation, the object that I loved beyond all things, my pleasure, my mind-altering substance, my soul food, my shrink. There is an often-quoted phrase from Albert Camus to the effect that everything he knows of man's existence, he owes to football. Everything I know about me, I owe to running the marathon.

I try to retain some semblance of proportion, reminding myself that my gift is for words, not strides, and telling myself that it is no shame to finish marathons closer to Hour Five than Hour Four. This time I'll just be the best runner I can be on the day. I'll run my own race, matching myself against people of my level of ability. Under no circumstances will I automatically accelerate whenever some male bimbo draws alongside me and pulls away with the heart-breaking fitness of youth. I will remind myself instead of the fat blob I was at 40, when I couldn't run upstairs, let alone 26 miles.

But it's no good. When it comes to marathons, I'm just a sad fantasist. This is always the year I'm going to be resolute and diligent about speedwork, find the perfect shoes (ones which will take two minutes twenty off the time it currently takes me to run a mile), do the 70 miles a week in training that will concertina my personal best by half an hour. Not that these mile-fixated weeks are necessary, apparently; someone's always ready with that marathon anecdote, the one about a friend who never went further than five miles in training yet still managed to finish in 3.30 while making £5,000 for charity into the bargain. 'Fantastic!' I lie, when I'm sick to hear it because I've been running three years now, been through ten pairs of shoes, done 20-mile long slow runs every second Sunday all through March and I still can't string together six 7-minute miles; no, let's make that three at 7.30.

The question I never ask myself is why I return again and again to my annual ritual of dashed hopes, this activity so unjustifiable in terms of time spent and profit earned, this thing that gives me blisters and bad knees. Reason doesn't come into it, though if pressed I could put up a pretty good argument for the way the marathon finds you out, confronts you with your worst self and gives insight into your best.

It's something to do with the distance. Twenty-six point two miles is just a spin in the car, or an energetic but pleasant bike ride. On foot it can be the journey to the cross. The human body is not designed to run that far. Twenty miles it can manage. When you're trained and sinewy and it's a fine spring day you can even enjoy it. But the extra 6.2 miles is where you weep and where you learn.

It's where all the deranged thoughts kick in: the violent impulses, the near-suicidal despair. Six more miles. On training nights, that's a little jog. In the marathon, tacked on the end of 20 jolting miles of hard road, you might as well be running to Australia. You never knew The Highway was the length of the M1. You can hate yourself, with your suddenly cumbersome body, your useless lungs and powerless heart.

In a bad marathon, primitive parts of your brain take over. You lose all sense of proportion or of self: what you stand for, where you come from and go to. You project your self-loathing onto the person in front of you. It's astonishing how much homicidal feeling can be generated by someone's backside. That's why they don't hand out machine guns at the 21-mile marker, only water and encouraging smiles. You're exhausted and dehydrated, one leg is numb, your shoes are shipping blood, you hurt and burn. You aren't running for a medal but for survival, chased by all your demons: fear of failure, ridicule, humiliation, of being caught by hellfire, an invading army, the Grim Reaper. Surrounded by thousands, you are on your own. You can't lie to yourself, or hide from the human being you really are. Your friends and family can only stand and watch. Only you can get yourself over that finish line.

But running a marathon is emotional food and drink. All running nourishes the soul as surely as it hones the body but the marathon is feast day: joy, gladness, rage, sorrow, despair, exhilaration, self-worth. It doesn't happen every time, or in the same place every year, but out in the long morning with 30,000 others can be that one-hour spell when you want to run for ever, in a place of peace and silence unregulated by the demands of the ordinary world. Waiting for you will be that last few hundred yards to your destination when your sweat-smeared gaze tries to fix on the clock and you know that in a minute or two you will cross the line and stand beaming and dripping while someone hangs a medal round your neck. Right at that minute, I swear it, I don't give a damn how long it has taken me. My bullshit and denial can come later, the little mental calculations and adjustments downwards: 'I'm allowed to knock off the five minutes I spent stuck behind the Wombles in Charlton'; 'I lost ten minutes queuing at the Evelyn Street toilets'. I am just happy to have got there and to have laid the burden down.

Some people think the London Marathon has got too big and unserious; it's not about runners any more, they say, it's more a festival for people dressed as waiters and characters from a comic book. That's their take on it. Me, I look at the sheer numbers who turn up to run it year after year in times that range from just over 2 hours to 8, 9 or even 30, and I marvel at what the human spirit can achieve.

I'll never know what it's like to play for Tottenham, or wear the yellow jersey or serve for the match on Centre Court. Running the London Marathon is the only chance I have to take part in a great sporting event. I am so proud of my medals. I hang them on a special hook on the wall above my desk so I can see them every day when I sit down to work. The memories that they conjure up inspire me. Even when I'm running the race, and I'm ten minutes down on my target time and not even over Tower Bridge yet, and my shins and cheeks are stung by the remorseless flak of a sudden sleet squall, and the part of me I use for messing things up and failing to follow through says, 'Go on, give up. What's the point? Go home and drown your sorrows,' another part of me, hungrier and bolder, says, 'I want my bloody medal!' Like the toddler I once was, banging her spoon on the high chair for dinner. It's not just a piece of tin, that medal, it's my reason for going on.

The Runners

Almost all marathoners, aside from those good enough to practise distance running as a career choice, are apt to look back on races run and wonder wistfully what they would have achieved if they had taken it up when younger, faster, slimmer, more supple or less burdened by demands of work, family and bank manager. It seems to me, though, that the marathon finds you only when you are ready to be found.

The reasons for taking on the 26.2-mile monster can be simple or complex, born of circumstances or forged of personality. For some it is a challenge that marks a significant birthday, or a celebration of recovery from addiction or illness, or a natural progression after a year or so's steadily less effortful jogging round the park. Or you move on to it because you're an elite athlete who's gone as high as you can go at the shorter distances. You do it because you want to get thinner and fitter, or because last year you did it in 4 hours and this year you're looking for 3.30, or because this year you might move into world class.

You do it because friends or workmates are doing it, or because everyone at your running club does it, or because you've watched it on the television and suddenly longed to be part of it, or because you want to run through the pain and stress of a broken relationship or unemployment or bereavement, or because you are a decent, sober, socially conscientious person who wants to raise funds for charity. My first London Marathon was an occupational hazard. The newspaper for which I worked had been given a bunch of guaranteed entries and as someone who never gets out of the room fast enough, I found myself volunteered. I was not to know then that running would become part of my life.

The idea for this book was simple: follow a bunch of runners of all kinds, from champion down to couch potato, through their experience of running London 99. I would find out where they'd come from to get to this point in their lives. I would ask why they were doing it *now* and hear about what they went through in training, and after they'd done it they would tell me what those 26.2 miles were like.

In these pages are the testimonies of all sorts: fast and slow, skinny and fat, able-bodied and disabled, young, middle-aged, 70-something, professional, elite, pretty damn good and snail-paced. Some run three or more marathons a year and some have never owned a pair of running shoes before. We all know about Everyman; this book's about Everyrunner.

The preponderance of Londoners in these pages may give the impression that entries for Britain's premier marathon are posted almost entirely from within the perimeter fence of the M25. I do know that at this minute someone in tights and Lifa vest is stepping out of a front door in Thurso, and that someone else is pounding along the minor roads of Suffolk or sharing the trail with a few pheasants in South Wales. I can only apologise to all of the thousands of runners the length and breadth of Britain whose efforts and insights have been ignored due to the dictates of time and proximity.

It is January 1999. We have all brought our dreams and demons, our ambitions and good intentions, hopes of glory or victory or at least of not finding ourselves wanting. We have entered a world of long weekend runs, of training schedules and carbohydrate drinks, of obsessive conversations about shoes and knees and times that are so profoundly boring to those we live and work with but of intense and intimate interest to fellow runners. We have embraced pasta and early nights, and put the cork back on the bottle of wine. Three months from now, on 18 April, we will bring the baggage of our lives outside the marathon and dump it for a few hours along with 30,000 others in the luggage trailers on the grass of Greenwich and Blackheath. We will get into our pens, next to world champions or clubmates or fun runners or Wombles, depending on our abilities. We may never see each other again, but for three or maybe eight hours of one Sunday morning in spring our lives will be joined when we run the last London Marathon of the twentieth century.

Chris Vernon was born in 1944 and has taken part in every London Marathon since 1983. He is a construction safety manager and lives in Dulwich, south London, with his wife, Sue. They have three adult sons and are both members of Dulwich Runners.

Chris Vernon's training log for 1–8 January 1999
1/1. Hyde Park 10k. Perfect weather. Felt OK for not running for 9 days. Miles: 7.01, 7.04, 7.05, 7.18, 7.07, 7.04. Last 0.2 – 1.09.
3/1. 12 miles. Sunday run with club. Knackered.
4/1. 6½ miles. Slow, tired. First day back at work. Cycled.
5/1. Gym. ½ hour.
6/1. 10 miles with Dulwich Runners.
7/1. Exercise bike ½ hour.
8/1. Yoga.

I came into running to run marathons. That was how it started. I was in the Round Table. Dinners. Charity. I jogged. I've always climbed mountains, spent a long time on my feet. Someone said to me, 'We've got three places for London, how about you, Chris?' So I reasoned, 'Well, I've walked 26 miles when I've climbed all those mountains, so I'll give it a go.'

I knew nothing about marathon running. I hadn't heard of it when the first London took place. I didn't know there were any other races. I thought the one when Jim Peters collapsed was the only marathon ever held. But I went and watched Hugh Jones win. I stood on the Embankment and saw people staggering all over the place. I'm a Londoner, I'll go to anything like that, a state funeral, anything.

I started training by running round the block and collapsing in a heap. Then I did it twice. Then I bought a book, *How to Run the Marathon*, by Cliff Temple. I couldn't keep up with the Get You Round schedule, which depressed me no end.

But I picked up a few hints and one Sunday I was doing the long run, as the book told me, and I met another runner who happened to be an acquaintance. I'd no idea he ran. So we ran along together. It turned out he'd done three marathons. I told him my fear that I wasn't going to get round. He said, 'If you can run a mile this fast this soon you'll have no trouble.' That made me feel much better.

All my training was by myself, by the book. I drove the routes in my car. I've still got all my training logs. Every step I've run since Day One. How far, how fast, every race. Still on the same tatty paper. Who I was beaten by. Who I beat. I don't go into reams. 'London Marathon 1990. Dream race. 1,584th in 2.55. First Dulwich Runners Vet. Wet at the start. Cold wind. Felt good all the way.' I've always kept it in the same form. The way Chris Temple said.

Your first marathon is one of the great emotional experiences. It compared with seeing my three sons born. I didn't know anyone else running. It was just me against the distance. Here it is: 'London 1983. Race. 3.44.' I didn't know much about what was going on. I forgot which mile was the last one. I was running along with tears streaming down my face. That said, I've done that on a number of occasions. That's how I know that's it. The wall. Any time from 18 to 21 miles.

After London 83, I wasn't going to go any further and here we are sixteen years later. For a long time I said there is only one race and that's London. Everything else is a training run. This one will be my seventeenth consecutively from 1983.

The best was obviously when I ran my PB (personal best) in 1990, because I was *so* prepared. Training had gone well. I was so focused. I had run that race in my head a hundred times. I knew the splits I was going to do. I knew them with my eyes shut. I was going to hit the button all the way through. Bang bang bang. It went like a dream. I just floated. I got to the Tower of London and saw my friend Keith. He put his thumbs up and said, 'PB?' I said, 'Yesss!', and who says that at the Tower of London?

One year I didn't have a particularly good run. I got through it and I got to the finish, but I was wandering round in a daze not knowing where I was, which is unusual for me. A doctor friend came up and said, 'Did you have a good marathon?'

I said, 'Malcolm, I don't know.'

He lifted up my eyelids and said, 'You prat, you're dehydrated.' He gave me a bottle of water and said, 'Sit down and drink that and I'll see you in the pub.'

Often you meet people you know early on in the race. You pull away from them, otherwise they'll pull away from you. You can't let that happen! Never!! Come on, you've been training six months for this race. It's a major part of your life. You have to be fairly competitive when you're a runner.

One year I met a training partner of mine, Colin. We'd run

all winter together, our long runs, Wednesday nights at the club, countless 10ks, half-marathons. We were great friends. You rarely see people you know that late in London. Either you've left them behind or they're in front of you. This was special.

I met him at 22 miles. I said, 'Hello,' and from then on nothing was said and it was a race to the finish. Nip and tuck. Legs like rubber at the bridge. Those were the days when it finished on Westminster Bridge. Turned up Northumberland Avenue, across Trafalgar Square, down The Mall, stride for stride. Neither of us looking at the other. Down Birdcage Walk and then, obviously, it was going to be a sprint for the line.

From Birdcage Walk there's a slight rise into Parliament Square. I was older than him and reckoned he might beat me if it came to a real sprint so I thought I'd test him on the hill up to Parliament Square. So he'd think, 'If Chris is going that far out he must be stronger.' I nearly collapsed. But I won. And we both beat three hours.

Since then I've always had the greatest respect for the guys who race it. It's not the same as racing against the clock. It was the fact that it wasn't only that we were going to break three hours, but that one of us was going to win.

But I think the marathon boom is over. The trouble with all running clubs is that we're all getting older. When I broke three hours for the first time in 1985, there were 2,500 broke three hours. Nowadays you're lucky if you get 1,500.

I see people now, the best in the club, who aren't as good as the ones ten years ago. The most competitive group was the seniors – U40 men. I was a 2.56 and I was the tenth best runner. Then as time went on it was the men in their 40s. Now it's the men in their 50s, and there aren't many in their 20s coming through.

You see that in all races. The people who were in the

running boom in the early 1980s are still there. I see the same people I was racing with 20 years ago. It's a bit sad! The sad thing is, I thought, 'When I hit 40 I'll win something.' And I never did. So I thought, 'When I hit 50 I'll win something.' And I never did. Because the same people were still in front of me. One of our runners, his father was a veteran; used to turn up for the championships every year and eventually it was a question of who was still alive. 'Old Harry's dead! Oh well, that's one gold medal gone.'

But it's the anticipation, isn't it? The whole build-up. The driving across Blackheath the week before to see if the Portaloos have been delivered. Waking up to Capital Radio saying, 'It's a beautiful morning on Blackheath.' The unpredictability of the weather conditions. You can be perfectly prepared, then wake up to 60 degrees. People have different impressions of the race depending on what time they run it in.

And it's the pre-race rituals. Honey sandwiches for breakfast. And why? Because Joyce Smith always had honey sandwiches. She said so in her book. She took her own bread and honey wherever she went. And then you tape certain toes, the ones that are prone to damage. The big toe on both feet. Like all marathoners I have no toenails. They just go black and drop off.

I broke three hours within two and a half years of starting from scratch. Comparing it with other people, I know many who can beat me at 10k with no difficulty who've struggled for years to break three. Long slow distance is what it's all about for me. I didn't start till I was 38. I wish I'd taken up running years before. I just wish I knew what I'd have done at 25.

Jessamy Calkin was born in 1959. At various stages in her career she has been a music journalist, tour manager, phone sex operator and Damon Hill's PR. She is now the features editor of the *Daily Telegraph* magazine and lives in Camberwell, south London, with her partner, Ralf, and daughter Alabama, known as Bam Bam. She dislikes physical exercise.

Ten years ago in New Orleans I met a guy called Chicken Man. 'Something bad will happen to you when you get home but it won't be too bad,' he said. 'Take this sachet.' Two days later I was back in England, doing a parachute jump for charity. Eight of us in a terribly small plane. I was sitting on the edge of this plane with no door, looking down. Very frightening. I jumped out.

I thought, 'I'll just turn and look around.' It was like being in a Fellini film. I turned back and saw him heading for me at great speed, this fifteen-stone guy. He crashed into me. The two parachutes tangled up together and we were plummeting to earth really fast. It was exactly the feeling when you have a bad dream and you think, 'I'm going to wake up soon.' And I realised I wasn't going to wake up. I was going to die . . .

I've always thought of the London Marathon as a traffic inconvenience. I've always said to myself, 'One thing I'll never, ever do is jog.' I used to see people jogging and be filled with contempt. My editor caught me in a tracksuit yesterday and said, 'Jessamy, what is happening to you? I always thought you were a respectable member of the lunching community and now look at you.' I felt worse than if I'd been caught snorting coke.

I never go on diets because it's like admitting you need to lose weight. I won't talk about going running because people might think I want to improve myself. It's a kind of indulgence. Undignified. The whole Bridget Jones self-deprecating thing, taking the piss out of yourself. I can't stand it. There's something narcissistic about it. I don't like people being incredibly in control, not getting pissed. When my friend Rachel offered me a place, the only reason I said yes was that I like the idea of having more energy. The same reasons I used to take speed.

The incongruousness appeals to me, too. People I've told have looked at me absolutely aghast. If you said, 'What's the least likely thing for Jessamy to do ever?' they'd say, 'Run a marathon.' Everyone in my office does it. They go to this horrible little gym like a hamster cage and look out of the window and sweat. Or they run round the Isle of Dogs. I feel like a giant squid that lives at the bottom of the sea.

When Winston Churchill was once asked why he'd lived so long, he said, 'No sports.' And I'm like that. I haven't found any sport which I liked. I've got quite short, muscly legs that look as though they should be good at something. I'm not a spindly wimp. My dad got to the Olympic trials at the long jump. My brother was rugger captain and in the athletics team. But even at school I hated it. I was in the table tennis team and the air rifle team, but I didn't consider them sports. I didn't envy sporty girls. I never wanted to be in teams. I didn't have the competitive thing.

In fact the only sport I *really* love is motor racing, the same way that I *really* love cars. I've had a Dodge Dart for fifteen years. It's done thousands of miles. I had a birthday party for it when it was 25. I invited all my mechanic friends and had it in a garden. People brought presents for it, like whitewall tyres.

I was brought up in South Africa. I was 9 when I went to school there. It wasn't a particularly good school so I was top of my class. Then I was sent to a progressive English prep school: co-ed, no uniform, incredibly glamorous headmaster and headmistress. I loved it there. I was there for two years and incredibly happy.

Then I went to a very straight all-girls public school which squashed all love of learning out of me. If you saw a boy in the road, you'd have to cross to the other side. I was expelled after three years for being an anarchist and a bad influence.

So then I went to a school with a reputation for being St Trinians. Girls walking round wearing bowler hats and clutching hot water bottles, teams of girls heading for the woods. I was a day girl. My brother was at school nearby in Salisbury and I discovered speed through him and his mates. I started supplying to other girls. I could tell my parents I was staying at school, and tell the school I was with my parents. I was really in town with the art school boys or at David Bowie concerts.

I got rumbled and expelled from there too. It was very traumatic for my parents because my brother was also expelled from art college and we had the police round with sniffer dogs. That was a bit of a blip in our relationship. The headmaster got a bit obsessed, too. He said, 'I'll see you in jail if it's the last thing I do.'

Off I went to school in Reading. I was there three weeks, then the drug squad arrived in my study and started stripping my mattress. They found speed. I was sent home. So no other school would take me and I had tutors from the local convent. They used to come to my house, a lovely old house in Wiltshire. We couldn't even find a school to let me take A levels.

But around that time my friend and I were going up to London on the train, and in our carriage was a man reading a book on Gladstone. He overheard me telling my friend how I'd been expelled and how I couldn't get to university and he put down his book and said, 'Anyone who's been expelled from three schools must have some talent. Come and work for me.' He turned out to be a Tory MP called Tony Baldry. He had a publishing firm. I stayed there for eight years.

My parents were really OK considering what I put them through. My brother was a heroin addict for years. He's been clean for seventeen now, and is an incredibly successful interior designer, living near Bath with a wife and four kids. But at the time I don't think my parents knew what they were dealing with. I've always felt that my mind and body were out of tune with one another. My mind is incredibly active but I'm physically quite lazy. I have bad concentration. Speed gave me focus. I didn't take it so I could go out and have a good time. In the end it made me very paranoid. I'm not like that normally, but it was like everything was everyone else's fault, not mine.

When I started working for the publishing company I was 18 and it was 1977: the punk era, the best times I remember. Three years ago I went to some club in Oxford Street which was full of 18-year-olds and I felt so sorry for them. They didn't have anything. Nothing to rebel against, nothing to do.

I lived in a squat near King's Cross with a punk rocker called Paul Grotesque. There were nine teenage boys living there, and me. I was the only one with a job. Stella Artois cans lined the living-room walls.

Someone left me some money, so I bought a Land Rover and went on a trip across the Sahara Desert with Paul Grotesque's sister and two couples including a pair of twin brothers who'd just come out of Eton and never left England before. Paul Grotesque's sister only went to get a suntan. None of us had driving licences; I learned to drive in the Sahara.

We were completely reckless and insisted on going on our own. At the other end, we discovered that loads of people go missing every year. By that time I was sleeping in a sleeping bag outside with no tent; that had gone mouldy. After six months we'd got as far as Ghana, where I met a garage mechanic with a 1959 Cadillac, the one with huge tail fins. I fell in love and said, 'I must have one of these cars.' So I rang my dad and borrowed the money to fly home.

Then I worked and saved up to go to the States. I went to journalism college, I was a cleaner for the Army and Navy in their books department (where I stole books), and when I got to the States I saw an advert for a 1961 Cadillac, which was perfect. It was 250 dollars. It belonged to a policeman and had a bullet hole through the windscreen. Everything was pink, even the steering wheel and key – a dirty rose pink, not horrible.

I bought it, drove it for three hours and then the engine blew up. I had to get it towed back to Washington. I couldn't afford a garage and a flat at the same time, so I rented a garage and lived in the car. When I got it back to England, I couldn't afford to repair it, even though I kept trying to get friendly with mechanics, so I sold it to a woman who remortgaged her house to pay for the repair. Which I thought was in the spirit of the car.

After I came back to England, I worked as a freelance music journalist and in a topless hostess bar at the same time. It was in Jermyn Street. They were both loathsome jobs. I went back to America as a tour manager and ended up staying there. I was 25 by then. I lived in Los Angeles and worked for the record company in the daytime and as a phone sex operator in the afternoon. I didn't do the calls, I took credit card details, except when I was really bored.

I had six months there and was beginning to worry about how I would get home when a former editor I'd worked for rang up and offered me another job, on a graphic design magazine. He paid for my flight and I worked with him for five years and lived in a council flat in Hackney. He co-managed Damon Hill when Hill was in motorbikes. I used to do his press and PR.

It was around ten years ago that I broke my back. I'd been seeing a therapist and I decided that what I needed was to do something I really didn't want to do. So I got involved in a parachute jump for charity.

After the fifteen-stone guy crashed into me, we got to 400 feet above the ground and pulled our emergency chutes. I got into the landing position and saw the ground coming towards me. I felt the pain going up, and continuing up my back. I'd fractured my eleventh vertebra. I remember lying on the ground and a guy driving up in a Land Rover. He said, 'Can you move your toes? OK, get in.'

I went to Maidstone Hospital. The surgeon who saw me had been trying to close down the parachute jumping unit. I was in the Silly Accident Ward with a footballer who'd fallen on a spoon and a girl whose foot had been run over by a bus. My muscles had been torn away, my whole diaphragm was swollen. I was off my feet for two months.

It slightly made me lose my nerve about things. Things I used to do as a matter of course – go-karting, rock-climbing – I didn't want to do them any more. I sued the parachute company on Legal Aid. It took five years, but we settled out of court for £25,000. That's what I bought my house in Camberwell with, so it all had a happy ending.

After I came out of hospital, I was still moving around from job to job. I lied my way into being Arts Editor on the *Tatler*, and after a year or so I was asked to do a world tour with a new band, and on that tour was Ralf. He was the roadie.

I did it because I wanted to go to Japan and Australia but it was hellish because I'm not organised at all. I was babysitting about sixteen people, basically, and it was a nightmare because I was hopeless. At the start I said, 'I'm not going to get drunk, I'm not going to sleep around, and I'm going to do the accounts every day.' I broke all these resolutions within 24 hours.

Ralf is German. Back then he didn't speak any English. I

met him in Berlin, the day before we left. I didn't know if it was going to last beyond the tour but it did. He learnt English. We were able to have conversations. Then I got a job with *GQ.* I loved it. I decided to move out of the Hackney council flat after someone got killed beside my car on a Saturday afternoon. We bought the house in Camberwell and six months later I got asked by *GQ* to go and write an article on learning to ski. So Ralf and I went.

There was nothing to do in the evenings and that's when Bam Bam was conceived. I was absolutely amazed. The only reason I knew was that my cousin came up to London to see me with her child. I was lying in bed thinking, 'Thank God I haven't got a child,' and then I thought, 'And I haven't had a period for a long time either.'

It was a huge time of soul-searching. Did I want to have a child, did I want to commit myself to Ralf for ever? Because I wouldn't have wanted to be a single parent. I didn't have a hole in my life to fill, there was no gap. My life was *great.* But I knew there would be no single right time. It's just that I felt I had to go through the process of rebelling against it, saying, 'Yes, I am going to go through with it,' 'No, I'm not going to keep it,' to help me make the right decision. And I've never regretted having Bam Bam. I knew that I wouldn't.

In a way, my life now is a bit too settled. Bam Bam is 3. I've got a mortgage. I work for the *Daily Telegraph,* which my parents have read all their lives, for God's sake. That's why I agreed to do this marathon. My friend Rachel said, 'You'll get fit, it'll change your life, you'll be a different person.'

But where is it? I'm waiting for some kind of enlightenment to come across me, when I'll bound out of bed or feel that I could run for ever instead of looking at my watch and thinking, 'When is this going to stop?' I'm going to Devon this weekend to stay with my parents. I'll run on my own for the first time. I've bought a talking book – Iris Murdoch, *A Severed Head*. I haven't run on my own so far because after fifteen minutes I want to go into a cafe and sit down. I'm like someone on a diet who's left alone with a bar of chocolate. I've never had any will power. I'm not going to get it now.

There are things I can be obsessive about, like cars, but the marathon is different. It's a physical challenge that you have to pull off. I'm not worried about not finishing things. My whole life is about not finishing. When I go running, and I do loathe it, my consolation is that I can always walk it. But I've agreed to do it so I will do it.

Though having said that, I've been doing my best to get out of it. I went to a cranial osteopath last week and was basically hoping he'd say, 'You're mad, you mustn't do that.' And my GP wouldn't play ball either. I told her she'd better check my heart because the ten years I spent on amphetamines might have put me in danger. She said, 'You've had a baby, haven't you? How long were you in labour? Forty-eight hours? Well, you can manage, then.'

Now my last hope is my ankle. I broke it three days before John Lennon died when I dropped my house keys into our basement and jumped down to pick them up onto what I thought was a pile of leaves but turned out to be builders' bricks. I'm staking everything on my ankle.

The fact is that the idea of people cheering me on and wearing a T-shirt with my name on it fills me with absolute repulsion. The number of people in the race puts me off. If 30,000 people want to do it, I don't. It's a kind of childish thing; I want to do something which no one else is going to do.

John Eusden was born in 1973. A promising athlete at school, he was offered training by both the British Ski Federation and the Lawn Tennis Association. Severely depressed after the death of his father, he gave up his job as a dollar sterling trader and since then has worked as an electrical contractor and a minicab driver. He lives in Loughton, Essex, with his wife, Nicky, and two children, Maisie and Joe. This is his first marathon.

> John Eusden's training log for the week commencing 18 January
> Day 1 10 mins easy, then 6 × 150–200m uphill, jog back.
> Day 2 3M easy
> Day 3 10 mins easy, then 1M brisk, 5 mins easy
> Day 4 2–3M easy
> Day 5 Race *or* 5–7M *or* 90 mins walk/jog
> (from the *Runner's World* Get You Round schedule,
>   devised by Bruce Tulloh)

I come from a big, close family. Friendly close, not fighting. Most weekends my cousins come down and there are twelve of us to Sunday dinner. People turn up at our house all the time. It's a lively household.

I was lively before my dad died. I still can be, but sometimes I have to force myself. I knew that if there was any sort of trouble, aggravation, I could go to my dad. Money problems, anything. When he died there was a big hole. I haven't done anything about that big hole. I've tried. Moving houses. A better car. Trying to replace him with material things as best I could. It hasn't worked.

I wasn't a kid when he died. I was 20. It's only now, seven years on and when I've become a dad myself, that I can look back and think, 'I was lucky to have with him what I did.' Seven years. It's took me all this time, and I'm still not quite there yet. I'm still feeling a bit small.

I'm the only boy. I've got three sisters. I'm the only Eusden in our family; Dad hadn't any brothers. It's a Danish name. If I hadn't had a son, the name would have finished. I feel I put pressure on Nicky when we started a family: 'If we have a girl this time, we've got to have a son next.'

Becoming a dad myself has meant responsibility. My first thought was, 'I've got to earn some money.' Financial responsibility. Being broke, I didn't really cope with it. I fell into depression. If you haven't got much money and you're around people who have you can start to feel inferior. Your whole body gets to you. You start to think, 'Look at me, I'm unfit, I'm overweight – and I've got no money.'

Now I've realised it's not about that. Well, it is to a certain extent, but you can have a laugh and enjoy your kids without loads of money. It's only now we've made the decision to sell our house, move somewhere smaller, that I feel I'm starting to take control of my life. I also think that if you feel good about yourself physically, the mental side of it comes easier. That's why I want to run this marathon. It's a mission. I want to get my weight down, get fit, so I can feel good about myself again.

I was a money broker in the City, a dollar sterling trader. I'd come there from working with my dad. He was a builder but he'd done other things, bits and pieces. Everyone always described him as a lovable rogue. He wasn't like Arthur Daley; he looks like a villainous type in his photo but he wasn't. He was very charismatic. When he walked into a room you knew it. You loved that – the friends who said to you, 'When I'm out with your dad, I feel I could do anything.' I still have people say to me now, 'We expect your dad to walk in behind you.' Seven years later it still feels like I've got to live up to it.

Three months after he died, the City job all got too much for me. I've been that low before, I've been suicidal. I think it's easy to institutionalise yourself when you're depressed. You can hide from the world. It's easy to go up to Goodmayes Hospital and say, 'I'm mad, this is where I live now.' You don't need no money. You can just sit there watching TV with all the other nutters.

I've gone there in my minicab to pick someone up. I've walked in and this man with a big *papier mâché* elephant mask he'd made was running towards me. The other nutters were all around him. It was like a film. A nurse said, 'Can I help you?' and I said, 'No, I'm just waiting for someone.' But as I said that, I thought, 'I quite like it here.' It was like a little world. No responsibility.

Soon as I was offered a marathon place I thought, 'Yeh, I'll do it.' I want to feel as though I've achieved something totally by myself, without anyone else's help. However I do it. Doesn't matter what time I do it in, I'm going to cross that finish line. If something goes wrong I'll crawl the last mile.

Because I have a habit of not following things through. I do one job one minute, then a different one. When I was in my teens, I loved tennis and skiing. I got invited to train with the British Ski Federation. I started tennis lessons at 10 and entering tournaments at 13. I was good, I got into one of the LTA junior training schemes. But the competitiveness started to get to me, everyone staring out in front of them when I just wanted to play for fun. So I didn't turn up for a tournament and then the LTA wrote me this letter, kicking me out. I didn't follow up the skiing thing either.

My three best mates laugh about it, me not finishing things. It's not a hurtful thing, but when people say that sort of thing to you, you get pigeonholed. You start a job and you think, 'When am I going to give it up?' With the marathon, you can be part of something that's so big but where no one's a loser. I want to love running. I don't want to be last, but I don't want it to be competitive. If I couldn't finish, I'd go into severe depression. 'Typical. What else is going to go wrong?' Just by finishing you're a winner. I want to be that winner.

Jayne Pope was born in 1956. An artist, she is also a partner in an interior design business. She took up running at 38 and two years ago qualified for elite status. She lives in Forest Gate, east London, and is a member of both the East End Road Runners and Dulwich Runners. She is an experienced marathoner.

> Jayne Pope's training schedule
> Mon. 1 hour easy
> Tue. 2 miles warm-up, pyramids, 2 miles warm-down
> Wed. a.m. 1 hour weights
> Wed. p.m. Dulwich Runners – 7–9 miles steady
> Thur. 2 miles jog, 12 × 200, 2 miles jog
> Fri. Day off
> Sat. 1 hour fartlek [walk/run]
> Sun. $1\frac{3}{4}$ hours or race

I came to London when I first left art college – I did graphic design. I've shown in Bond Street and Wapping, sold in Cork Street, can you believe. Now I've started in business too, interior design.

I was brought up on a boat on the Hamble. We always lived on boats; my dad used to do them up. When I was 6 we went to live in South Wales, by the sea. In Pembrokeshire, which was absolutely wonderful.

We were English and they were all Welsh so I always felt a little bit outside of it. I think that's where my competitiveness came in, because I felt an outsider. You didn't belong, so the only way in was to get into the teams. The rounders team, the gymnastic team, the hockey team. I was in all those and I tried to be the best. It was the same with exams, I thought I'd better do a little bit more there too, so I had to try and be top of the class.

My dad was a property developer. I get on well with him

now. I never used to. I didn't speak to him for years. They divorced when I was 26. I love them both now they're apart.

My nutritionist said to me, 'Runners can be obsessive.' You get a lot of borderline anorexics. When I'm running, I don't like to think of anything else. I get into a state of meditation. That was why I took it up in the first place. I was 38. I'd just finished a relationship. I'd always done circuits and cycled to work, and when the relationship finished I felt inadequate, weak, very sad, very lonely. I was a freelance and work had dried up. I was very vulnerable. And then I found the East End Road Runners, and they were brilliant. At last I felt a sense of belonging.

I got stronger and stronger through running because it gives you confidence. The other day, *Vogue* rang up Sarah, my business partner, and me. They asked us, 'What is modern seductiveness?' I said, 'It's being true to yourself and confident,' and that's what you get through running. Being at one. No one but you there. You aren't wearing anything. You're in motion and running. When I get home I feel liberated. Running is sexy. Runners themselves aren't, not the men; that's what's so sad about it. But we don't do it for other people to look at us. We do it for ourselves, to feel great and sexy.

I ran my first London Marathon in 1995 with three friends from East End Road Runners and did 4.34.05. I was doing it for my dad. To get back at him! He said that, not me. At the end of the day I walked back to meet him in the reception area and he said, 'What did you do?' I told him and he said, 'That wasn't very good, was it?' Now my best is 3.12.24. It's all down to training. That's me, I need to have something to show people. I need something to work against.

Running was something I did with everyone else. The first inkling I had that something was good was when I did the

Benfleet 15 one year. I finished and thought, 'Where's everyone else?' I'd come third and I was so shocked.

It was a slow progression. After the first London Marathon I started running with Roy at East End Road Runners rather than my three friends. It was to push me, because I felt I was being held back slightly – I think we were all holding each other back because we've all gone on to do much faster times. Strangely enough, my times went down in every marathon I did after my first till eventually I thought, 'Right, maybe I could qualify for the elite.' To be an elite woman you have to run 3.15 or under and two years ago, in November 1997, in Berlin, I did 3.12.24.

I've never kept a running log. I was saying to a friend of mine that I did really well in the Finchley 20 last year, two minutes off my time, and he ran off and looked up his own time on e-mail so he could come back and tell me, 'Last year I did so-and-so.' I can't see the point. Why look back and say, 'Oh, I felt shit on this date this time last year'? I remember! I remember every single Finchley run. I don't need miles and miles of books. I don't need any more clutter.

Last year I did four marathons from April to April. I had to walk from 21 miles in the last one, I'd had enough. It was too much. I did not want to do it, I'd done it so many times. I thought, 'I'll get to 21 miles and feel crap.' And that happened. But I still did 3.25! Ego, ego. And I feel quite excited this time, emotionally and physically stronger.

Elite women start in Greenwich Park at 9.00. They lay on fabulous facilities for elite runners, but there's an awful lot of elite women who run with the crowd because what you miss running with the elite is overtaking people. And the championship men flood past you, which is demoralising. And they do tend to go off incredibly fast, the elite women. Usually I get up to $6\frac{1}{2}$-minute miling in the first mile, which is ridiculous. It's really too serious. No fun. No bands. I'll just keep it to 7-minute miling so I'll have more energy at the end.

On marathons, I'm prepared. I eat well. I know that the first 3 or 4 miles will be really nice and that at 20, 21, you're going to have it tough. Emotionally, you push yourself to the limits. A friend said that at 24 miles she burst into tears and thought, 'I can't go any further.' And she was doing a fabulous time.

A painting of my marathons would just be blurred shapes. Very blurred, because your whole mind becomes slightly blank. As you start out the colours are very bright and near to the finish they fade because you don't see so sharply.

The bit that I dread will be going down The Mall. More spectators, more cheering. It doesn't work because you feel so dead, it's shattering, you're exhausted. The more they cheer, the more you want them to shut up. They don't say 'Well done' to you because they expect you to do well. You're just given a medal and you go through.

Mark Hudspith was born in 1969 and his brother **Ian** in 1970. They are among the top long-distance runners in the UK. They live in Fawdon, Newcastle-upon-Tyne, with their parents, Eddie and Pat. Following in their father's footsteps, they run for Morpeth Harriers. Mark works part-time as an accountant and receives funding from the National Lottery. Ian is a teacher. Their coach is Jim Allder, former Commonwealth Games marathon champion. This will be Mark's eighth marathon, and Ian's first.

The Hudspith brothers' training schedule
   Monday through Friday: Morning – 40/45 mins steady
   Monday p.m.: Club night. 10 miles fartlek
   Tuesday p.m.: Recovery run, 9/10 miles steady
   Wednesday p.m.: Midweek long run. 15/16 miles

Thursday p.m.: Track night with Jim Allder. Longer reps on track, e.g. $8 \times \frac{1}{2}$ mile

Friday p.m.: Recovery run. 7/8 miles

Saturday a.m.: Recovery run. 7/8 $6\frac{1}{2}$-minute miles

Saturday p.m.: Race or road session

Sunday a.m.: Long, slow, steady plod. $2\frac{1}{2}$ hours minimum

Sunday p.m.: 30 mins very slow

'Over 1,000 runners set off from Morpeth on New Year's Day for a 14.35 mile journey to Newcastle.

This race was being run for the 84th time, and brothers Ian and Mark Hudspith shared the pace before settling in with a sprint, Ian narrowly getting the verdict with a time of 1.13.29.'

From *Runner's World*, April 1999

Ian: I started running at primary school; the first race I remember was in the Newcastle City Schools. But we both mainly played football then, we didn't take the running seriously. We were quite good footballers and used running just to keep us fit, though we were both in the Harriers from about 11.

I probably started training every day when I was 14, maybe having one rest day a week. I started going along to Jim Allder when I was about 15 and then I started to take it progressively more seriously till by the time I was at Liverpool University I was training every day.

Mark: My first race was in the Newcastle City Schools too, though in those days there wasn't much time for running. I had a similar sort of progression to Ian – I took it seriously from 16 and asked Jim Allder if I could join his group for track training. I was experimenting, really – 1,000 metres, 1,500 metres – to see what I could do.

Ian: I think even then it was inevitable, with a coach who'd run marathons, that we'd do the same. Neither of us was quick enough to be as good at middle distance.

We got to know Jimmy through our dad. He was a runner with Benwell Harriers but they folded so Jimmy asked him to join Morpeth because they were short of runners. He and Jimmy used to run together.

This is my debut marathon. I was doing 5,000 metres, 10,000 metres on the track. I had a good season two seasons ago but last year didn't go so well and I always had it in my mind to run a marathon. I lived in London for a few years, teaching in Enfield and living with my girlfriend, but we split up so I came back here. Moving back and living with Mark, I thought, 'I'll give it a bash.'

Mark: We've both got jobs. 'Professional athlete' suggests to me that you do it for a living, but that's not the case. We make a living from our jobs. I've run eight marathons, had some success and won some decent money but obviously you cannot run a lot of top-class marathons in one year. I've worked part time for the past two years and that's made a big difference; my running was on the slide with work commitments and accountancy exams. It's not that I'm doing more training; I'm just getting more rest. It's definitely made a difference.

Ian: Mark's getting a little bit of help through the National Lottery and hopefully I might receive some funding soon. But it won't be enough to pack my job in. You're talking £2–3,000 and that's nowhere near enough.

Mark: I think we're both very regimented about our training. We've got a set routine and stick to that.

Ian: I'm not that obsessive. I don't keep a training diary.

29

With our living together, 95 per cent of our London Marathon training we'll do together. We keep each other going. There are mornings when you don't feel like getting up because you're really tired but with Mark getting up you don't want to feel you're losing out.

It's twice a day; even when we're doing a low-key race we'll train in the mornings. One of the worst things is when you go to a nightclub and at twelve o'clock when everyone's ready to go on till two you have to say, 'Sorry, I've got to go, I'm doing a long run in the morning.'

We get on. We always have. Even when we were younger, we never used to fight. Apart from at snooker. Mark was better than me. Really smarmy around the table. I used to flip my lid. But we're good mates. We've got the same friends, mostly from school and running, we go on holiday, we go to Newcastle games together, we've got the same interests. Be difficult if we didn't get on.

Mark: Ian's probably more extrovert than I am. Bigmouth. I'm a lot quieter, more reserved. He's a bit more instantaneous with his reactions whereas I'll stand back and think first.

Ian: But we've both got reputations for the never-say-die spirit. I definitely get more frustrated, though. If I do a bad session, I'll fly off the handle.

Mark: We're both aiming for the qualifying time for the world championships: 2.14. There's also a team qualifier of 2.16. We're averaging 120 miles a week in training, and it's not very nice. The worst bit is probably the long runs. They're just monotonous. Sometimes you can just get up and think, 'This is going to be a chore.' But it's got to be done.

My motivation is the races themselves. I think it's the

competitive element of it. Just trying to pit yourself against other people.

Ian: I like racing. I like all of it really. I like the sessions, I like the long steady runs, I look forward to going out on a run. I like running, really.

Mark: I haven't got any toenails.

Ian: Mine are fine.

Helen Spriggs was born in Scunthorpe in 1974. At 13 she was diagnosed as diabetic. This is her third London Marathon and she has also run New York twice. She runs using a Bayer Diagnostics Glucometer Esprit that enables her to monitor her blood glucose level without having to stop. She works for the British Diabetic Association as its youth services co-ordinator and lives in Earls Court with her boyfriend Nayim.

I was a cross-country runner with my school. I've always been one of those people who's a tortoise. Give it a go, even if I don't come in the top five, the top ten. I've got this mental strength to keep going.

I went to school in Winterton, which is not a very well known place. Where I actually lived was a little village called Flixborough. They had that big chemical disaster before I was born, at the works. It wiped out a lot of it. There were two generations, one that had always lived there and lost relatives, and a second generation who moved there when they rebuilt the lost houses.

It was a little place, only one pub, no shops and only two bus services a day to Scunthorpe. Couldn't be further removed from where I live now. Growing up there, we used to spend our time running and biking and my father, who's a

really keen walker, introduced me to the Great Outdoors.
My dad and I were very close. Still are. He's a self-employed
television and video repair man. My mum's a nurse at
Scunthorpe Hospital. I'm an only child.

I did the Three Peaks of Yorkshire when I was 11 – Pen y
Ghent, Wearnside and Ingleborough. My dad had only taken
me up there to do one, Pen y Ghent, but I got really taken by
it and didn't want to stop. So we did the next one, and we
came back, and within another month we did all three, in
hellish conditions. When I did the New York Marathon in
1997 in the same cutting rain I remembered doing the
Peaks, when after two my dad was ready to give up and I
said, 'No, let's go on.'

I was diagnosed diabetic on 9 January 1987 at approximately 11.30 a.m. You never forget. The whole Christmas
period, I had really terrible flu symptoms like nothing I'd
ever had before. The thirst I had, I could drink three Cokes
in a row. Family and friends came to the house and Mum
said, 'Don't be drinking all that stuff, wait till everyone's
here,' and I'd feel so guilty. I'd be getting all these two-litre
bottles of Coke when they weren't looking. I felt I was being
greedy.

I was constantly passing urine. I could be sitting on the
toilet and drinking at the same time. Drinking it with it
coming out the other end. You just could not quench that
thirst. And I lost so much weight. I was becoming a skeleton.
And having that kind of flu – I wasn't myself. I was, like,
tired. Not bubbly and energetic. I was just totally changed.

Just before Christmas, in *Just 17*, I'd read about a girl who
had diabetes and I thought, 'That's what I've got.' In one
sense it was a relief. You knew that something was not right
and it wasn't normal. The thirst, it just dominated your life.
At the same time, it was a really big fear. Your mind said,
'Don't be silly, it's not really as serious as that.' I showed the

Just 17 article to the family and they brushed it off: 'No, you're all right, you're all right.'

This went on for three weeks. I returned to school. I remember being in an art lesson. The teacher said to me, 'Change the water,' and I drank it instead, this water that had been there for years in this filthy, paint-ridden cup.

The teacher must have said something because soon after that my dad took me to the GP. In some way I kind of knew already. Looking back some time after I'd been diagnosed I remembered that when I was 7 one of my favourite books was *Sugar Mouse*. It was about a girl and her dog who were both diagnosed as diabetic, and it was really strange; I loved that book. It was as though I'd known my fate deep down.

I remember the doctor's face. That confirmed it before he even said anything. When he did say it, I looked over to my dad. It was really powerful to be told. Told that I was going to have to take injections for the rest of my life.

It's sort of blanked out now, but I remember being in shock. There was my dad grasping at straws: 'Couldn't she take tablets?' There was the doctor informing the hospital I was going to be admitted. There was us, driving home. My dad saying, 'Eat something,' and passing me a banana. And him and me looking at each other before I said, 'I don't know if I can eat this now.' My mum getting back from her hair appointment. Walking out of the car with not a care in the world to be faced with this.

Off I went to the hospital. You were bombarded with information then. It was, like, you spent a week learning everything about diabetes. Management of it has changed tremendously since then, but I remember now a nurse coming up with a syringe and a phial of insulin to inject me and I said, 'If I've got to do this for the rest of my life I'll do this one now.' And I've done it ever since.

I think it was my way of taking control, taking a grip. At

13 I suddenly became much more independent than my peers. I had maturity and responsibility. Although my parents learned all about it as well, I wanted to have control. I wanted to be in charge. It was my diabetes, and I think the strength I showed helped my parents through it.

Maybe even early on, right from diagnosis, I felt I had something to prove. It's like a chip on your shoulder. The first year or two with it was like living hell. You didn't have a life. It was timetabled for you. You couldn't lie in, you had to inject at a certain time, eat half an hour later. If you left it even ten minutes you felt you were going to fall on the floor; it was that inflexible and regimented. You were forever testing your blood, having snacks. In PE at school you were frightened to exert yourself because you knew it was going to directly affect your glucose level. You feared having a hypo, which happens if you've missed a snack or exercised without adjusting your insulin or diet.

Feeling different from your peers, that was awful. Now, looking back, I feel that in some ways I liked it because I gained a little bit of respect and attention: injecting myself, when everyone else at school was terrified because the tetanus woman was coming. But very soon it became a drag. Your life and personality develop and change between 13 and 15. You wanted to be out with your friends, but if you even just went to McDonalds they could eat any time and you had to sit there with a Diet Coke. I remember trying to explain it to schoolfriends. I had a glass of milk near me and I said, 'This is no longer milk, it's medicine.' It was like food was totally taken away from me as food.

Seventeen is when you first start going out drinking with your friends. I felt I had to drink more, stay out later. When I left home, went to university, that was my rebellion time. Seventeen, eighteen, nineteen. I never told anyone I had diabetes. I would inject in the toilet. I was covert about it.

I was living in a Hall of Residence when I first met Nayim, my boyfriend. In the end I left my insulin vial and syringe out purposely so he'd see it and it would spark the discussion. So he'd think it was something far more serious, like I was a junkie. I told him the very minimum, not a full textbook rundown. It was a gradual process. He'd notice how I was managing it, he was very inquisitive. I'd take him to my clinic appointment. He wanted to accept it and understand it as part of me.

He's lived with diabetes and me for seven years now, longer than my parents have. He can tell by looking at me if things are wrong: if I become pale, if my eyes cloud over or lose something, if I become quiet or extremely over the top. Aggressive, that's how I get. It's a similar feeling to hitting the wall.

When I started running it was a totally new experience, and in particular a total relearning about my diabetes. All those years of watching it on telly in Flixborough, you never thought it was accessible. I couldn't run a mile when I first did it. I had all the determination but I didn't have the ability.

When I was first starting out, on those one- or two-mile runs, it was like, 'Oh, I'm going to be fine. I can just follow the general advice.' It was when I started running five nights a week that I began to realise I was having a lot of delayed hypos. I'd get in, and four or five hours later I'd drop. And when I really upped the distance to an hour, an hour and a half, I was forever up and down.

I went to my hospital team and said, 'I'm going to run a marathon,' and my consultant said, 'That's impossible.' And that was like a red rag to a bull. On my second visit, when they knew there was no way I was *not* going to do it, it was frustrating for them because they weren't able to answer my questions. And for me, not being in control again was really very frightening. For nine years I'd had it, I'd been very comfortable, confident; diabetes was nothing major, it was second nature. Suddenly it was *dominating* my life. People say it's the running, the marathon, that takes over. For me, it was the diabetes.

Everything was trial and error. I was really so determined. I had to personally organise the whole of my regime. I'd be testing six times a day. When I was in my rebellion stage I wouldn't test for weeks. Now I was like a pin cushion.

I finished my first London Marathon in six and a half hours. My last marathon was New York and I did 5.54. I loved it but I was disappointed with my time. I felt if you loved something that much you should nurture it, give it as much of your life as you could. I felt I'd let this thing down. Should I give up now and be proud of what I've done? But I couldn't be proud because I thought I'd let it down. It's such a passion. It feels like a person. I felt I hadn't given it my best and I wanted to.

I always run marathons on my own. You're there. You're among thousands of people. You identify with everybody. But it's one of the loneliest of times because there's only you who can get you over that finish line, and I mirror that to my diabetes; you've got your family, healthcare team, friends, but it's only you who has the diabetes, it's only you who can control it.

Kev Wood was born in Macclesfield in 1957. He is a social worker. He lives in Greenwich, south-east London, and is men's captain of Dulwich Runners. This is his second London Marathon.

I grew up in the North-West where I went to the local grammar school. Both of my parents worked in the Health Service. My father was a nurse, my mother as well. I'm an only child.

I suppose it was a time of great freedom, and a fair

amount of opportunity. Saturday jobs were easy to find. I worked in a hardware shop. And so money could be obtained through honesty and hard work. In terms of running, I really enjoyed cross-country but not track and field. I simply wasn't properly advised by the teacher responsible. He turned training into an absolute chore. Three times a week. Never said why. I think he understood the principles of training but didn't explain the purpose of it.

The puzzling thing was that during training I'd compete with boys from other forms and they'd beat me because I was tired. So I slipped away. Then I discovered girls and drink and enjoying myself. I did A levels and then went to live in Cardiff and did a degree in Eng. Lit. Seventy-eight-ish. Didn't do much in the way of sporting activity there. When my finals came along I went back to a limited amount of running because it helped to clear my head. And then I moved to London, initially for six months, but I'm still here.

I was living in Blackheath at the time of the first London Marathon, at the end of the road. I went to look at it and took the camera. I seem to recall that it was really quite impressive. It wasn't what it is today. There were only 7,000 people in it. But still a hell of a lot of people passing by for ages and ages.

It didn't encourage me to run at all. I didn't link myself with it. *Then* I thought that people who were capable of doing marathons were incredibly fit, super athletes really. And of course at the time there wasn't quite the element of mass participation. But certainly I took the view that anyone who could complete a marathon would have to be an extremely fit and gifted athlete.

I'd been training then for five years, but I was doing karate. That was a good training discipline. Initially on graduating I'd thought about teaching, but I got a job with Lewisham social services for eighteen months. Then I decided to qualify as a social worker and since 1983 I've specialised in working with young offenders.

Much of my work is in the court system. That goes along with the skills needed to relate to the people. To them the bad guys are the police. We're turning up and offering them something that might keep them out of custody. After fifteen years of working I now do fairly complicated things which could have thrown me on Day One. I have to manage quite difficult situations but onc becomes used to it. One of the prime things I bring, I suppose, is a sense of calm. Unflappability.

I find it really helpful to use running as a means of dissipating any stress. Time to think. Sometimes I do go through work issues. Run them through. You can unravel quite complicated things. Put them into their box. They don't matter. Well, there are other things that matter more.

I reached a stage with the karate where I wanted to stop, really, replace it with something else. There were political problems within the club, and it had been five years. I didn't want to lose my fitness, so, as I was living in Lewisham at the time, I started off on one lap of Hillyfields. I can't remember the first race I entered. Might have been a 10k or something. Certainly I could see myself improving a little bit. That helped to motivate me. Plus, although it was after the height of the marathon boom, running was still practised a lot more widely than it is today. More runners on the streets.

I entered races reasonably regularly; nine or ten a year. Clocked up a couple of half-marathons. I ran quite a bit with a friend. I prepared for my first marathon as a non-club runner. I can't remember exactly what motivated me apart from having gone to the start every year. It is quite a sight to see.

I wasn't really sure what time I was aiming at. Under four hours, I suppose. I didn't do nearly enough miles, to be honest. I think I peaked at 55/60. I don't even know if I've still got the training log. In the week leading up to the start, like many other people I developed a psychosomatic cold. I can remember queuing up at the herbalist's in Walworth Road. They gave me a bottle of something foul and horrible which I placed great faith in. Probably full of ephedrine or something. I remember covering my chest in Vick's on the Saturday night and thinking, 'I'll probably do it and if it kills me, so be it.' Completely gone by the morning. Of my own making. No substance to it.

I remember getting to Greenwich. My partner at the time, she had a stall at Greenwich Market. I was looking out for her but I didn't see her. I remember passing a team of police officers in helmets in Deptford. They were being roundly booed. I got to the halfway point and felt pretty good. Like many beginners, I'd probably set a PB for the marathon at that point.

At the Isle of Dogs, which is everyone's low point, I decided to turn it into my own territory. A place where I felt strong and comfortable. I remember coming out of the Isle of Dogs. I was starting to feel quite tired. There was someone banging away on an Irish drum, a bodhran. That encouraged me because my mum was Irish, that spurred me on. There was a low point heading towards Wapping, but I got to St Katharine's Dock and friends were there and that was good. I was dreading the cobbles but it didn't seem to matter much. I remember getting towards the finish, the Embankment. Friends called out, encouraged me. The finish was on Westminster Bridge. We threaded round Parliament Square and I was overtaken by a waiter.

Through *Runner's World* I'd agreed to take part in some research that Bart's were doing in the incidence of the common cold. After the race they provided a recovery area. They wanted a blood sample and I'm so squeamish I had to lie down for half an hour. My friends thought something serious had happened because they'd seen me going past looking strong.

I ran with Dulwich for a couple of years, had a break while I was doing a management course, rejoined around 1992. I started to train regularly and decided I'd give running a real go. Certainly the marathon wasn't a priority for years. In some ways I was a bit scathing about it. I thought London was such a big event, one which encouraged lots of non-runners. Almost devalued the efforts of proper runners. People in fancy dress, people who jog around. Aspects of London devalue running in general. Your TV pics showing people collapsing over the line, people walking. As a dedicated club runner I felt it was a bit of a shop window for that sort of sport. And as men's captain at Dulwich Runners I've very much resisted the marathon as the main activity. I think people have accepted that there is more to running than gearing up to run the London Marathon. I've done a hell of a lot of running between my last marathon and this one. I tried to increase my speed over 10k. Didn't really set the world alight but it satisfied me. Then I got injured in 1995 and I've had an Achilles problem ever since. My speedwork is limited now, I can't do the work to improve. But running longer distances slightly more slowly seemed OK.

As regards this year's time, I'll tell you that in eleven weeks. I'm going to sit on the fence on that one. I've got a number of targets. I'll tell you if I achieve one.

Flo Gibson was born in 1955 in the East End of London, and is the proprietor of an ironing service. She has been running for four years and is a member of the East End Road Runners. She lives in Newham with her younger son, Jay, and her partner, Bob, who also has a place for London. This is Flo's third London Marathon, and she has also run Florida.

Monday: Rest
Tuesday: Club. Track. 5 miles
Wednesday: Circuits. (Running equivalent – 5 miles)
Thursday: Club. Short Woolwich, the other girls
wanted to get back. 6 miles
Friday: Park. 6 miles
Saturday: Rest
Sunday: Race. 15 miles

There was only one place given out to our club this year.
They usually put it in a ballot but this time they thought it'd
be unfair because somebody might pick it out who'd hardly
been there. So I got it because I had the highest attendance.

I had the highest attendance because I find running really
hard and I just think if I don't turn up I'll find it even harder
when I go back. But though it's hard I do it for the sense of
achievement. It's about passing your son on the track. And
since I've been running I've never felt better physically or
mentally.

I suffered from depression as a child, believe it or not. It
was due to insecurity, being as my parents split up. I was 5.
There were seven of us, I was in the middle. You're not the
firstborn and you're not the baby.

I was very clingy, frightened to be on my own. I didn't
want the door shut, didn't want the light off. That was a
horrible feeling but I didn't know what it was about till
afterwards. I just used to feel scared. At 15 I took an
overdose and went to the doctor's and he gave me anti-
depressants. It used to come about once a year, in the winter.

I left home at 16. Only a baby, really, but I thought I was
a woman, grown up. I got married the day after I was 18 so I
didn't have to ask for consent. We lived in King's Lynn. I had
my first son at 19 and my second two years later and had
postnatal depression both times. It just felt the same. After
the second pregnancy, I attempted suicide again. Cut my

wrists. I didn't want to wake up with that depression. I just couldn't see an end to it. My husband left when my second was six weeks old and I went to see a counsellor. On the second visit she suggested that my fear was about being left alone, and now I was alone, and I'd coped. I felt stronger for it. It's funny when your fears themselves are more frightening than what you're afraid of. But I still like company when I run.

I got a cleaning job a fortnight after I had Jay. At a chemical factory. The only reason I got the job was that they'd had a big explosion the week before and everyone had left. When I was 22, I moved from King's Lynn back to London. I used to drink neat Scotch first thing in the morning. I worked in a pub. I just used to drink all day, till the early hours, because we went clubbing afterwards.

I worked in those pubs and clubs for about three years, and I smoked 60 cigarettes a day. To make ends meet, I sewed beads on dress fronts, and I hate sewing. I glued leather on heels, getting high on the glue. I did cleaning. Then when the boys went to school I went back to my old job, which was typing.

One day Jay, the youngest, saw an advert on TV about people dying of heart disease through smoking. He said, 'If you died, who could be our mum?' I just stopped. I didn't smoke another cigarette. I also gave up the drink because I couldn't have a drink without a cigarette.

At the time I had a partner called John. I met him when I was working at the pub. We lived together fourteen years. We saved up to get a house. But he was a drinker, he used to come in drunk. We moved into our house and he lost his job. I was doing three jobs at the same time to pay the bills. Friend's pub till lunchtime, typing in the afternoon, come home and do dinner, then the nightclub. I was earning it and he was drinking it.

The office where I did the typing was really quiet. I don't

like sitting still. I started going to hairdressing school but when John and I split up, hairdressing wasn't enough. And my hands used to shake when I was holding the scissors. Around that time my dad died, and I went to see a hypnotherapist-psychotherapist about my lack of confidence. Once a week for a year. He used to say I could do anything if I put my mind to it.

That was nine years ago. After I went to him, I got a job at the Ideal Home Exhibition, demonstrating ironing presses in front of thousands of people. I remember going up the elevator to the exhibition thinking, 'I can't do this,' and I heard his voice saying, 'You can do anything you want.' First week I earned a thousand pounds in commissions. We sold ironing presses to people who were doing an ironing service, and I used to pick their brains. Now I'm the proprietor of one myself. I started with a secondhand iron and board and these days I've got two girls working for me.

I've been running for four years. I wanted to do it before, but I thought it was all elite runners in a running club. But then I saw an article on the East End Road Runners in our local newspaper. It was about people running the London Marathon who when they'd first started couldn't run round the track. I joined the club with the intention of being able to run a mile, because that seems so far when you can't reach the end of the road.

My first London was in 1997. I did 5.24. I was really excited, felt like this big star. It was all advertised on radio, everyone was talking about it and I was taking part. I felt so proud. Never thought I'd run a marathon, it was always something you went to watch. I've got a photograph. My face is all lit up as I cross the finish line.

I could be having a bad day, then go running and all the problems get into perspective. I've said I find running hard, but I like knowing that anyone out there who isn't a runner wouldn't be able to compete with me. I took Jay out once.

We ran a $6\frac{1}{2}$-mile circuit of Canning Town and I said, 'Do you want to do another?' He said, 'No, I'm going home.' I went off to do another and he said, 'Mum, you're amazing.' I'd like to be running in my 80s. It's good for your bones.

I ran London again last year and knocked 34 minutes off my time, but I trained much harder, with track sessions and circuits. This year I'd like to do sub-4.30. Actually, this year I think I'd like a new pair of legs, if I'm realistic.

Tony Evans was born in 1969. He lives in west London with his wife Sam and sons Billy and Ashley. In 1996 a 30-foot fall from a roof left him paralysed and in a coma. When he woke up he swore that one day he would run the London Marathon.

Before I fell I was taking drugs, I was in and out of trouble, always fighting at weekends, thieving, in and out of prison. I did a two-year, a six months and a three months, all for the same reasons. I was in and out of cash-in-hand jobs. I'd been addicted for about ten years. My mum always said I had an addictive personality: drugs, drinking, puffing.

The night I actually fell, I was drunk. Loads of cocaine. I was about 30 foot up, trying to get into a friend's house. The drainpipe collapsed. I went through a partition which broke my fall but spun me round on my head. The guy who saved me by keeping me awake, he's now dead. Through drugs.

I was in a coma six, seven weeks. Came out, didn't know anyone, didn't understand anything, didn't know how to talk. I was basically having to learn everything from scratch again: the ABC, how to eat, how to move my arms. I couldn't walk or balance my head. If I wasn't leaning against a wall I'd fall sideways. And apparently around that time, I saw the London Marathon on the telly and because I couldn't move my arms or talk properly I said to my little brother as a joke, 'I'm going to run that.'

I had to be told that I was a drug user because I forgot that's what I was. Once I was told, I did remember. I was, like, '*Bloody hell*!' The time I was in a coma, it did wean me off, there was that about it.

So I went into the rehab unit at Northwick Park Hospital and they seemed to pinpoint my problems. They made me walk every day, and I tried to run round the hospital, and it took me a good 40 minutes for something that should have taken five. When I came home I was still sleeping all day. Still couldn't understand anything.

They tried to get me into counselling but I needed answers to the way I was feeling now, not for what might have happened when I was a kid. And the way I was feeling now was aggressive. I was angry at not being able to hang a picture on a wall. Anyone can hang a picture on a wall, and I couldn't.

I went to Rehab UK, which is for people with brain injury. To see what the problems were and learn ways of going round them. They try and get you back into work. It helped me a lot. And fifteen months from when I had the fall I was approached by a psychologist called Frances. She asked would I come back to Northwick Park Hospital and do a seminar in front of the nurses about what happened to me, how I've managed to get well in such a short space of time. I did it with a lot of confidence. And two weeks before the marathon I'm due to give a seminar to Paul Boateng and his cronies, all about the accident I had and how Rehab UK helped me.

I start a college course in three weeks, a BTech Diploma in Sports Science. I'm hoping that I can work with people like me, who've fell off roofs, been in car crashes, people who've had brain injury and want to get fit again. If someone turns to me and says, 'What do *you* know about it?' I can say, 'I *do*

45

know.' It's all down to Rehab UK, they showed me how to get my confidence back. So I'm running the marathon for them and Northwick Park Hospital. Half and half.

It was difficult at first. It's hard to breathe because I've got a tracheostomy. I can't drink and run at the same time. I've got to concentrate on swallowing. I've got a delayed swallow. I've had ten months to train for it and sometimes I've felt I've bitten off more than I can chew. I used to get in a temper. I'd go running and get to the point of being unable to open my mouth when I got back in again. I don't do that now.

Originally I wanted to do the marathon in under six. Now my goal is under four. The guy I'm running it with is a teacher at Rehab UK, a veteran. We went on a run with the RAF – all up hills to see if I had the stamina. It's only been 20 months since I fell. He keeps telling me, 'Don't push your goal too far. Just to finish is good enough.' So I try to keep that in the back of my mind.

I've been with Sam thirteen years, we met at a party. For years I said I'd never get married. I just didn't feel all the palaver of getting married was for me. Once I'd had the fall and came round and saw all she'd done for me, I thought, 'Why haven't I married her before?' She made all the arrangements while I was in the hospital. I came out, got married after a week, came home, fell asleep. It might sound horrible but my two sons and Sam used to come in third, fourth place. I'd put drink, drugs, going out first. Now she comes first, the kids come first, I work my life round them.

When you've been one side of the fence and come back on the other side, it's a very thin line between you and the old life. Even now I say to Sam, 'I'm always around it.' Every day. When I got out for an hour and a half with my friends, I can tell – everyone in and out of the toilet. I end up coming home. It's not that easy for me to say, 'No, I have to leave now.' But as soon as I see drugs, I have to go. I read an article about Elton John; seven years after he come off it, he can go to a party and see drinks, drugs, OK, but as soon as he sees cocaine he has to come home.

I was lucky enough for the kids not to have noticed how I was before. All they're seeing is this guy who runs and has got time for them. Not, 'My dad takes drugs.' I was the worst role model in the world for them. Now there's no drinking, no smoking, no drugs comes in this house. I can't explain the way I feel, but it's great. There's no way it's going to get me again – I'm totally in control of that.

All the pain and hurt I caused certain people still brings me out in a cold sweat. I got christened after my fall. I got my kids christened. There's got to be some reason I was given a second chance: to do some good and put things right. I want to go into schools and tell kids. It's not easy. On drugs, I was happy. Drugs was easy. If someone said, 'Stop,' I'd say, 'Get out.' But then look where it got me.

I just really want to run this marathon. As I go over that finish line, 20 months after people were saying, 'You might not walk, you might be a vegetable,' it's going to be very emotional. The old brain doesn't forgive easy but I'll have done something not many people have done and I'll have got my fitness back, better than it was before. Once I can get over that line, I can say, 'I am better.'

Karen Hutchings was born in Okehampton, Devon, in 1965. She lives and runs in Barking, Essex, with her partner, John. She is a national account manager for Swissair and a member of East End Road Runners. She runs several marathons a year.

I didn't know I'd got a marathon place till quite recently, and just after I heard I was off skiing in Switzerland for three weeks. I'm still wavering at the moment; 'Shall I do it or not?' I've put on weight because I haven't been training as much as usual. The last marathon I did was Chicago in October so it's not that long ago, thankfully. But it's realistic to know I can't do $7\frac{1}{2}$-minute miling this time. Take it steadier. Pace myself. I always go off too fast.

My first London Marathon was in 1992. I don't have the photo up because it's so dreadful. In training, my idea of 18 miles was actually about 10. I finished in 4.52. I was sponsored by West Ham so I wore their kit. Got asked to get my tits out for the boys round the Millwall area.

Going up to watch my mum's friend from Devon in 1991 was how it started. My mum turned round and said, 'You could do that.' I played squash twice a week, I wasn't particularly overweight, but certainly in 1995 when I next did it I'd gone down two sizes in clothes. I felt so much better about myself. So much more confidence. All down to the weight loss.

I joined the running club in 1994, and it was key. Meeting so many people who had the same interests. I was married at the time, and the running helped when I wasn't happy at home. I'd found a hobby. Something I really enjoyed. It's not a dress rehearsal, life. You're here once. I lost a close friend I worked with at 32, and I just think you've got to give it your best shot first time round because you're not going to get a second chance.

I spent more and more time at the club. John and I started up as running partners and then partnered up properly in 1997. It was down to meeting someone who had the same interests, something my other half didn't want to do. You don't realise how running can take over your life.

There's lots of marital strife at the club. I'd say, of the people I know, four had problems or are having them. I'm absolutely convinced that people who take up running feel better about themselves and realise that what they have at home is not what they want. I'm sure the losing weight factor helps. I was a size 14 who went to under a size 10. It's running that gives you that little shove. What's fascinating is the number of females who've gone through the same experience.

Training for a marathon is definitely lonely. First London I was on my own, plodding the streets for two or three hours. You can pass the time a lot quicker with someone else there. I got so close to Judith and Trish from the club when we were training together. When my marriage got shaky, they were the two people to call on.

My other half and I had been together ten years, married two of them. We should have split up instead of getting married, but I didn't have the guts to do it then. My wedding dress was almost a size 16. I didn't like the fact that the 14 was too tight and I had to have a size 16 wedding dress and have it taken in. I shouldn't have done it. But when he asked me, I didn't have the guts to say, 'No, let's wait.' Because if you've been together seven years already how much longer do you need?

John is a desktop publisher. He's into computers big time. He was a boxer and a motocross and BMX racer. He's made me stricter in my sport because he's very disciplined in his. Very disciplined but very injured. Seven years of sports clinics. He's in a huge amount of pain, but he wants to run because I run.

Florida 97, we did the first half in 1.36. I was flying. Then I got an upset stomach and he went past me when I was in the loo. But in Chicago we ran and finished together. It's great because you've got someone you want to be with – to give that big hug and kiss to at the end.

It's got its bad points. You complain more when you're with someone you know than when you're with a stranger. But on the other hand you know when the other's feeling down, you know when they're hurting. If we ever do halfs or 10ks we always finish together. Not so much the marathon because you train for the personal best, but the majority we finish together, certainly.

Tushar Patel came to England in 1991 with his parents. He was born in Madras in 1978 and now lives in Fulham. He is in his first year of a degree course in business information technology at London Guildhall University. He has raced London twice, Manchester and New York. His wheelchair is valued at £4,000 and is supplied by Whizz-Kidz, a registered charity which provides tailor-made mobility aids such as wheelchairs, tricycles and walking frames for disabled children.

Tushar Patel's training schedule
Mon. Track. Sprint distances
Tue. Gym
Wed. Track. Long
Thur. Swim
Fri. Track. Sprint – long
Sat. Gym
Sun. Long session. 13–18–26 miles

Wheelchair racing is a prototype of cycling: the Tour de France. What tends to happen is exactly the same. While the cyclist in front is battling, the draught at the back is helping the others. If you don't take your turn at the front after two miles everyone gets around you and starts nagging you. We do the same thing, except in a wheelchair. The wheelchair is the bicycle.

I got polio when I was 2. I can feel my legs. I can put pressure on them. I can kneel on them. There's no restriction apart from I can't walk on them. My dad knew a bit about wheelchair racing and when we were in India he always said, 'When we get to England I'll put you into it,' because he knew ever since I was little that I was competitive.

When I was 13 I went to Grove Park School in Kingsbury and the physio took notice of how actively I did basketball. He had two racing wheelchairs, one of them not being used, and he thought of me, how it might be a good idea to put me in a marathon and see what happened. So I was lucky in a way. I got into the right place and I got people to give me chairs.

They started taking me to the local park at lunch to train, and getting the PE teacher to help. I did two races in that chair. It was a completely different shape to what I've got now, a bucket, a square thing, four wheels. The wheels were so small compared to your normal day chair. A hundred p.s.i. in the tyres. You didn't have to put so much power into it as a normal chair. It just rolled off basically. It felt easy.

When I was 15, I did my first mini-marathon with the aim of winning it. The first competition you do, you don't know anything about racing, you don't really know why you're there. The whistle went, I blasted off, and after the first mile I just died. I went in to win and I didn't and everyone was trying to comfort me, and it basically didn't do it for me because I didn't win. I came fourth.

I went away comparing my time with the winner's and thinking, 'OK, six minutes to catch up, so I'll train harder.' Four times a week in the park. I had to persuade all the teachers to give up their lunchtimes because there had to be someone there with you the whole time. By the time I was 16 and up for my second mini-marathon I'd managed to get a second chair from my club, Falcon Wheelchair Racing Club, and the great thing was that this other guy who'd won the mini-marathon was a member, so I could keep track of him.

They lent me his old chair and that was great because I had specialist equipment to race in, I had a lot more chance to win. I got into this habit. I wouldn't let anyone pass me. I wouldn't have it. I found it horrible. I got into all sorts of crashes. Once I went to warm up and there were hurdles on the track; I was feeling so good powering my chair along that I went into the hurdles. 'What are you doing?' they said. 'Are you trying to jump hurdles now?'

In my second mini-marathon I came second. I was 20 seconds off the winning time but I won the 14–18 age group. A great feeling. My first ever trophy. I've still got it. That inspired me to get more into racing. I started going all over England: Leeds, Cardiff, Newcastle, Sheffield; mini-marathons, 10ks, half-marathons. Back at school I met Whizz-Kidz, and the physio asked them to sponsor a racing chair. Now I'm on my second one from them.

When I got the first, it was great. I thought, 'I've got my own chair. I'm not borrowing anyone else's. It's built for me. No excuses now.' But I didn't know anything about training. I was going out and doing the same thing: 6 miles on the track, 13–18 miles on the road. With wheelchairs you have to be more careful and with all my crashes they wouldn't let me on the road at first, not till they'd got the confidence that I wasn't going to crash any more.

I was 17 when I did my first ever half-marathon. At Portsmouth. It was great because though most of the competitors had never seen me before, some of them already knew of me. 'Stay away from him,' they were saying. 'He's going to shoot off.' That made me feel good. Must have been something I was doing right.

I came in sixth or seventh. The top athletes, they go into the finish line and immediately compare their times with other races they've done. They take account of the course, they look at the conditions. I didn't know anything about that, the technical side. I didn't start to get the hang of it till I did races myself and got more interested in the way they analysed things. When you experienced it yourself, it made sense.

My first London Marathon was at 18. You've got to have

done a certain time to get in but my coach put in a good word and I got selected. My aim was tenth place and a good time. I'd never been through the experience. The course. The cobbles. I hit the wall, but luckily I had someone to work with. There were three of us. I didn't have enough in me to sprint at the finish, and I was aiming at the wrong finish and I put all my energy into that when the guy behind me shouted, 'This one!' and got in there just before me. So I lost my tenth place by two seconds. But I did 1.52 – still my personal best.

Last year I was going for tenth place again, and after two miles I crashed. Twenty m.p.h. in a wheelchair, roundabout, sharp turn. I had the chair lying on top of me. Supporters aren't allowed on the course: I was lying there for two minutes. Then I shouted, 'Come on, somebody help me up!' Bad race. But I did 1.56 and I managed to beat the bloke who crashed into me. I was surprised to see him at 20 miles. When he came in, he wouldn't look at me.

To be honest, when I'm in a race, all the time I'm looking at other people round me. I prefer getting nervous: you start to feel uncomfortable on the start line, you just want to go. Predicting what's going to happen next, sudden mind changes, what are they going to do. Things you should be paying attention to before the start, like warming up and stretches, I tend not to do, but now I stay a bit more focused before a race because if you haven't warmed up, it's really hard after 22 miles to keep your arms moving. You have to smack yourself a couple of times. 'Get moving!'

The wall tends to hit me around 23–24 miles. It changes depending on what sort of training I've done. If you're not working with someone your speed drops from 4-minute miles to 6 or 7. There's no one to pull you away. If you've got someone with you, you just stay there, you don't talk yourself out of it. Other athletes might be different; this is me. Lazy bugger.

Racing chairs cost so much money, if you want the top equipment. Mine has carbon-fibre wheels and an aircraft aluminium frame. It has to be part of your body. If you don't feel comfortable it's going to be hard, it might get in the way of what you want to achieve. I've got a computer for pace, distance and speed, and brakes just like a bike's. Before, my chairs didn't have brakes so when it came to stopping just like that it was a bit of a problem. The wheel front's 21 inches. That's long. I've probably got the longest arm length in racing. I'm almost built for the sport.

Caroline Taraskevics was born in Edinburgh just after Christmas 1958. She has two children, Sarah and Kathleen, by her first husband, the rock singer Phil Lynott. She lives in the West Country with David, her second husband, and they have a daughter, Natasha, and a son, Lukas. This is her first marathon.

To:
The Features Editor,
The Daily Telegraph,
1 Canada Square,
Canary Wharf,
London E14 5AR

November 1998

Dear Sir,
I understand you are offering readers the chance to join your London Marathon team to raise money for The British Brain & Spine Foundation, and I'm writing because I would really like to be part of it. I'm approaching forty and totally committed to getting fit

and have already started training, although I only took up running this year.

The charity is one that means a lot to me because I lost my father as a result of a serious head injury following a car crash. I was astonished and full of admiration for the work done by the brain surgeons and their team, the intensive care nurses, the physios and all the other staff who helped him in his all too brief recovery, and I would be proud to take part in this race in memory of his name.

Yours,
Caroline Taraskevics

There was a whole-page feature in the *Daily Telegraph* and I sat on it for about a week and then I wrote the letter. I was in my workshop making fairy wings when they rang and told me I'd been accepted in the team. I just screamed and went leaping around the place. 'I've been *accepted*!' I was ecstatic, because by then I was thinking it wasn't going to happen. And since that day I've trained and trained.

I'm the third child of five, the child of someone very famous, now dead, an entertainer called Leslie Crowther. I was a very wayward teenager, the sort of teenager nobody wants to have. I went to St Paul's School where I was a small fish in a big pond and left early. I was very interested in acting, and very rebellious. I worked in a number of jobs and ended up deliberately in the music business.

At 16 I did a nude photo session on my parents' bed, wearing my grandmother's silk embroidered jacket and nothing else. She was quite a woman. They told me it was only going to be printed in foreign mags but it ended up on the cover of a men's magazine here. That shows you how naive I was. Silly, really.

I was desperately seeking attention, and I also believed at

that time, in my innocence, that experience created maturity and the more bizarre the experience the more likely you were to become super-mature. When a job in the music business was suggested to me it seemed like the answer to my prayers: drug-taking, self-abuse, associating with glamorous people. I made one or two really good friends and that was where I met my first husband, who was a musician, Phil Lynott. We had two children together, got married, took a lot of drugs and loved and hated one another in equal parts, and it was a pretty rocky road. And then I left him and went back home, and eighteen months later he died.

At the time I went home, I stopped taking every sort of mind-altering substance and have never taken them since. Most of the time it's been a huge improvement in the quality of my life but sometimes there's been a great temptation. And sometimes I've resented the fact that I haven't got an escape route.

I've done a variety of things. I've fallen in love again, married and had two more children. I had a go at running my own business, which is coming to a close now, and I've done some work on getting happy. Last year when I saw the London Marathon on television, it just lit a tiny little spark. I thought, 'I'm going to be 40 next year. I'm going to do that.'

I've been a very irregular exerciser, to my constant frustration. So initially I thought that if I give myself a really huge goal I will have to focus and make exercise a part of my life. I had a very bad relationship with myself, the way I looked. I thought I was overweight and unattractive. I couldn't really reconcile the way I felt about myself with what other people said. 'But you're fine.' Etc.

And I knew it was sad that I was coming up to 40 and still didn't like myself, the way I looked. I wanted to embrace myself, my whole self. So I started running, I started going to the gym, and it started to make a difference.

I don't mind running on my own for long periods. I pass the time by redecorating my house inside my head. I sometimes think, 'What am I doing? Dull, dull, dull,' but I have to put that out of my mind because after 10 miles you'd stop. The two things that wake me up in the night are a horror of injury and a vaguer horror of not being able to compete. I see clips of the marathon on TV and I think, 'My God, I'm *included* in that. That is really fucking amazing.' I get quite buoyed up about that. And the flipside is absolute panic.

I am resolving my feelings about my body as a result of this. There have been two huge bonuses I didn't expect. I've learned to accept the way that I look and it isn't the unrealistic expectation, the body I see in a magazine; it's me, I like it, it's a healthy me.

And I feel *great*. There's a quotation I love – don't ask me who said it, but it goes, 'I wake at dawn with a winged heart and give thanks for another day of living.' The doors in our house have latches and a few years ago when my youngest child was 3, you'd hear his fingers on the latch of the bedroom door and you'd say, 'Who's that?'

He'd say, 'It's *me*!' And he'd come running in with this huge grin on his face, and I'd look at him and think, 'I want to feel like you in the morning.' And I do now, and that is just worth everything and that is what is going to make me continue. It's part of my whole being now.

Steve Wehrle was born in 1948 and lives in Crystal Palace with his wife Anne and young son Matthew. He works for the publishing division of the BBC and is chairman of both Dulwich Runners and the BBC Running Club. He has run every London Marathon.

NAME: Steve Wehrle
YEAR: 1999
TRAINING WEEK: Week ending 10/1
M. 5
T. 5 inc. 6 × 2 mins fast
W. 7
Th. 5 inc. 1 6.02
F. 7
S. –
Sun. 11
TOTAL: 40

I got to 30 in 1978 and I hadn't done any sport for twelve years. The beer belly had started. I ran for a bus one night, 200 metres, and it took me the rest of the bus journey to recover. I thought, 'Why am I so unfit? I'd better do something about it.'

I was living in East Dulwich at the time. I started doing one lap of Peckham Rye and coming back home again. A mile or so twice a week. I discovered a guy at work was doing the same things so we started meeting at the Ladywell running track, the pair of us, on a Thursday. It was just before the jogging boom and we got a lot of derogatory comments, kids shouting, people sounding their car horns.

Then I read in the paper that there was some possibility of a London Marathon and I said to my colleague, 'I'm going to have a go at that.'

'How far is it?'

'Twenty-six miles.'

He said, 'You can do it if you want to, but I'm not.'

I didn't have a clue what to do in training because I didn't belong to a club. No one to talk to. Magazines like *Runner's World* didn't exist. We didn't know what sort of mileage we ought to be doing, what sort of pace. It was hit and miss. Twenty-eight miles a week for two months.

I did 3.52, that first London. There were some 6,000 people in it. I was just overjoyed to finish and I had no intention of running any more of them. But *Runner's World* came out, and the new-breed clubs started. I decided to do it again and every year which followed it became, 'OK, I'll try again.'

My fastest was in 1991. Brilliant. The easiest marathon I've ever done. The weather was perfect. I hadn't got injured. I never suffered at all. I never hit the wall. I ran the last 10k in just under 44 minutes. I remember the countdown to the finish. Forty-five seconds to break three. Six of us going hell for leather over Westminster Bridge. I ducked under three hours after years of 3.10, 3.11. Just a perfect year.

There was another year when I made a real mess of it. First 5 miles in 33 minutes, took me 72 minutes to do the last 10k. It was absolute hell. There were people coming past me in Northumberland Avenue who looked terrible. But they were passing me. Another year I got cramp like I've never had cramp before. This side of Westminster Bridge, I was just standing there. People screaming like crazy, and I couldn't move.

One year I didn't know I was running till two or three days beforehand. I went down to the London Marathon exhibition. A colleague took me over to Mel Batty, Eamonn Martin's coach. 'You want to run?' he said, and just opened his briefcase and gave me a number. I found out on a Thursday and ran on a Sunday.

People say, 'You must know the course backwards,' but you don't. On the day, there's so many people either side of the course you don't see any of it; you could be anywhere. The year I ran badly, I purposely ran in the middle of the road because I couldn't stand the noise of the crowd. When you're a bit dehydrated or not feeling good, towards the end seems like forever. You get confused by the mile markers. 'Did I just pass 18? I'm sure I've run 22.' Being experienced doesn't necessarily stop you doing silly things. One of the guys at our club, a guy who knew what he was doing, bought a pair of shoes on the Thursday before the marathon and ran in them. He couldn't believe he'd done that. Six blisters.

I leave a second pair of shoes with Dulwich Runners support group. They usually stand at about 13 miles, then move through to the 21-mile point. Three or four years now, I've changed my shoes at 21 miles. It gives me a mental boost. Sit on the side for 30 seconds, change my shoes and set off again.

I got faster from the age of 30 to 44. Over the next few years, I slowed down a bit. I've had injuries, though luckily not many. The worst really was five years ago. I got a problem at the base of my spine: some degeneration at the bottom disc. I have to say that before that I never stretched. Now it's three days a week in the gym and 20 to 30 minutes of dedicated stretches. Runner's stretches, yoga, the sun posture, shoulder stands. As long as I do those, I seem to be all right.

I did 4.15 last year because I ran it with a girl from the club. I took over as chairman of BBC Runners thirteen years ago. I'm very proud to be receiving an award next month because the membership has gone up from 40 to 70 this year. Younger guys don't seem that interested but younger ladies do.

If I can do 3.29 this year, I'll be pleased. I'm so pleased I've found something that I enjoy doing and it was the right time in life to find it. Socially, there've been some great times. I don't feel 50, most of the time. And I've kept a count; I've run nearly 30,000 miles since I started. Once round the world and a bit more than that.

Sophie Mirman was born in England of French parents in 1956. After beginning her career in the typing pool of Marks & Spencer, she went on to found Tie Rack and then the Sock Shop. After selling on the company in 1990, she started the children's clothing company Trotters, which has two shops and a mail order division. She lives in south-west London with her husband Richard Ross and their three children. This is her first marathon.

We've got a problem and we need your help.

It all started last year one Sunday morning in April. We were watching the London Marathon and foolishly challenged Mum to take part. Now as you know, our Mum, who you may know as Sophie Mirman or Sophie Ross, has a reputation of being strong-willed and never one to turn down a challenge. So, since April, our normally sensible, rational mother has been pounding the pavement with a vengeance. The problem is coming before us. Dad is doing the cooking and so we are being starved. Food wise as well as emotionally.

As part of the challenge we have also had to make huge sacrifices. Pocket money is going towards sponsorship and even Oscar the dog has sacrificed his bones. So where do you fit into all this? Well, to make our sacrifice more bearable and to ease Mum's swollen feet, we are determined to raise lots of money. Our target is £10,000.

Our chosen charity is the Starlight Children's Foundation which is a charity dedicated to brightening the lives of seriously ill children throughout the UK. This includes the granting of wishes to those children who may be sick or dying. They also provide entertainment in hospitals by arranging ward parties and outings. This is such a wonderful charity that by raising a lot of money, our sacrifices and eating Dad's cooking will be more bearable, so please give as much as you can afford.

Mum has promised that this will be her last mad moment before slipping quietly into middle age. Do ease her path with your generous support.

Love,

Natasha, William and Victoria Ross

Last year, the children were watching the marathon on television, and I thought of the challenge of training and then the challenge of completing it, and of all the different people running it, and I said, 'I want to run that.'

The children said, 'Come on, do it. Do it for a charity.' My husband is very involved with the Starlight Foundation, and the children said they'd sponsor me one month's pocket money each, and Victoria, the 5-year-old, went up to her piggy bank and came back with 4p. So I said, 'OK, as long as I can find a friend who'll run it with me.' And unfortunately the first person I asked said, 'Yes.'

Polly, my friend, and I went along to Run and Become to buy my first pair of running shoes. I was in my business suit. I thought I was just going to buy a pair of trainers, but the assistant said, 'You've got to run to the bollard at the top of the street, and back again.' Fifty metres. I came back wheezing. Seven runs to the bollard and back again later, I had the right shoes.

I find it absolute agony. I'm not at all athletic. I was never good at running at school, never. I was good at languages, not sport. The only race I ever ran was the Hyde Park Fun Run. Two and a half miles. I did the race on crutches because I'd had a knee cartilege operation three weeks before. The two blokes behind me were determined to finish last, so they had to carry me over the line. I have done no sport since my first daughter was born. For twelve years I've done nothing. A year ago I had an operation on my foot, so I thought the doctor would be bound to say no. And nothing came of my knee trouble either. So I've gone down every avenue.

The first time I ran I did a half circuit of the park. I was wheezing, bent in half. I couldn't take another step. I had a problem with the shoes; they got a bit dirty so I put them in the washing machine. Then I started getting serious blisters, and three weeks later I discovered that the front of the shoes had collapsed and my feet were hitting the bump. My poor feet. So I bought another pair of shoes. At the end of four hours of running, exactly the same thing had happened. One foot was bleeding.

And it's hard. It's a real juggling act and with three children it is very tough to fit it all in. The dog doesn't like running either. We go down to the New Forest quite a lot, and I took the dog for a run with me there, and he disappeared. When I came back he was on the doorstep looking reproachful.

Every joint in my body is aching. I discovered I had a problem with high blood pressure. I feel an awful lot fitter now, but it has cost a lot from the point of view of my feet and joints. I mumble when I run because I get very angry. About the whole stupidity of the situation. I have conversations with myself because nobody can answer back. Or I listen to the radio; I discovered *The Archers* the other morning. I keep thinking that I must be insane to be doing this. Richmond Park has completely lost its charm. By the second circuit, I hate it. Even the deer stare: 'Oh, her again.' Polly had a hysterectomy in October. Then she had a dislocated hip. And she still runs faster than I do.

It's a fairly huge event. I look at it in awe. I find it a very scary thing to be taking on, because I still don't have the confidence I can do it. Every long run I go on, I can't sleep the night before because I think I'm not going to do it.

Once I've done it, that's it. Definitely. I might continue running, but only for one hour at a time, not four, five, six or however long the marathon is going to be. The longer I go, the more everything hurts. I can't run fast. I have absolutely no expectations. I think I am probably quite competitive but I'm not viewing the marathon with any competitiveness whatsoever because I know it's going to take me a very long time.

Max Jones was born in Handsworth, Birmingham, in 1927 and worked for ICI until his retirement. He was a Cambridge running Blue and as an ultra-runner holds several world records in his age category. He is a member of Birchfield Harriers and Valley Striders, and team coach for Age Concern. He has run every London Marathon so far, and the 1999 race will be his 100th marathon. He lives in Leeds with his youngest daughter, Sue, and her family.

Max's Minimum Marathon Method
   (from Age Concern's *Coachnotes with Max Jones*, reprinted with Max's kind permission)

Many of you here today will be taking part in your first marathon on April 18th. I chose my words carefully because there are three types of marathoners: those who race, those who run and those who, er, take part. It goes without saying – but I'll say it nevertheless – that it would not be a London Marathon as we know it, with 5 hours' television coverage entertaining 6,000,000 viewers, without the 20,000 whom many of you represent.

The central problem of the marathon is not the distance, it's the speed you go at in the first half which is the overriding factor, whether you're racing, running or just having a fun day on the streets of London. It is *not* a condition of entry that you run every step of the way; it is far more important, particularly if you're a first-timer, that you finish so that you can collect your medal and all that lovely cash which your friends are going to stump up for Age Concern.

Max's Minimum Marathon Method has no hills, no 400m repeats, no Fartlek, no Long Slow Distance runs. All I do now is run, 'flat out', 4 miles over the same road course, not less than 3 times a week, not more than 5, and I race at least twice a month, preferably 4 times. Let me make it quite clear, though, I am *not* saying don't go for a 20-mile run if that's what you look forward to on a Sunday with your friends in the Club. What I am saying is that I don't believe it will reduce your marathon race time by a single minute, let alone the minute per mile – and more – which my method has done for me . . .

I was raised in Handsworth in what would now politely be called terraced houses, and I went to boarding school because my father and mother divorced in 1935 when I was 8 and it was easier for my father to look after one child (my older sister) than two.

I was very fortunate because the school I went to was super. It was tremendous. I'd no idea what was going on between my parents. My sister knew more than I did. It just washed all over me. I remember when my mother left that she was 'going on holiday'. It just wasn't the sort of thing people did in those days.

The guy who founded this little prep school was Sir Milsom Rees, one of the physicians to George V. He inaugurated scholarships for the sons of members of the diplomatic service, barristers and civil servants. I don't suppose for a minute he thought the Deputy Chief Collector of Taxes would see this advertisement for scholarship applications in the *Civil Service Home Journal.*

But my father and I went down to Sir Milsom's rooms in Wimpole Street. I'd no idea, I didn't know Harley Street, let alone Wimpole. The maximum age for taking the scholarship was ten, and I was ten on the day of the examination. Mr Upwood, the headmaster, was invigilating. Because my father knew a bit about arithmetic and we'd played arithmetic games together, I knew numbers. I remember finishing the paper after 20 minutes and staring about, and Mr Upwood coming round and saying, 'Anything wrong?' I enjoyed it at boarding school. I fitted in well.

After the war, I went straight to Clare College, Cambridge, without having to do national service because I had a state scholarship. Approximately 90 per cent of the students there were returned servicemen, so as little more than a schoolboy I found playing soccer against them was fairly hard and I turned to running. I ran in the college team. We didn't have a coach, we just did what we thought we ought to do. We just ran. We knew nothing of intervals. Occasionally Old Blues would come down to talk to us but there was nothing structured at all. We went for runs, and those who happened quite by chance to be 'gifted' came out on top.

Having had some success at school (I'm just rationalising) I presumed that running over fields was the way to train, and I got myself into the second team against Oxford in December 1946. That was where I first met Roger Bannister. It was my course, I knew where I was going, he didn't. I was first, he was second. I crossed the finishing line and the chairman of the Cambridge University Hare and Hounds Club, the Reverend C. E. Wood, apologised most profusely because the stopwatch was broken so I wasn't given a time.

The following year I concentrated entirely on cross-country runs versus Oxford. I ran in the first team that year. Chris Brasher and I were the two best runners in the club and we crossed the line together. Unfortunately, four Oxford men crossed the line together in front of us. So I said to Chris Brasher, 'With Roger Bannister far quicker than us in the mile, and the other guys quicker in the 3,000 metres, I think we ought to go for the steeplechase.'

I ran it once, in the Midland Counties Steeplechase Championships, and it was awful. I was almost literally climbing over barriers at the finish. Whereas young Brasher went on to win gold in Melbourne in 1956. In the meantime, our paths rather diverged. After he finished fifth and I finished first in the next term's trials I didn't meet him again till after the first London Marathon.

I met Pam when she came up to Birmingham. My father-in-law had been born in Sheffield; they'd emigrated to London before the war. Then in 1958 there was a merger between the Yorkshire copperworks and the corresponding pieces of the metals division and I came up here to Leeds with the merger. My father-in-law was horrified. 'Leeds? You're taking Pam up to Leeds? In the First World War we hated them more than the Germans.'

After I got married, I more or less stopped running. I did no sport apart from watching it. I keep telling the class runners at our club, 'Get yourselves organised. Family comes first, work comes second, running sixth or seventh. Prioritise.' Though as my family says, I'm not only emaciated, I'm obsessed. Just as well I've got a thick skin.

I was still happily working at ICI when I finally retired in 1988. Pam's father, who died in 1984, was twelve years older than his wife and as he got into his 90s and she got into her 80s she prevailed upon Pam . . . she wouldn't move up here to Leeds so Pam had to move down there. Pam's mother died three years ago, by which time my daughter Sue and her family were up here, and Pam has friends and a sister down there. . . . But we're still together. I'd prefer her to be here. But there you are.

I ran my first London Marathon just to support my old mate Chris Brasher in his new venture, and because running a marathon was the thing to do. So I could then die happy. I *was* 53, remember. So I ran the London Marathon and was rather pleased with myself to have beaten four hours, although I was nearly an hour behind Brasher, which did peeve me a bit.

Out of curiosity, six weeks later I bought *Running*

magazine to see the results. They were in chronological order. I was a little put out to find I was 4,428th out of 6,500 finishers. When I was young in 1948 I ran in the inaugural English cross-country junior championships in Sheffield; I'd been fourth overall so 33 years later I thought to myself, 'There won't be many 50-year-olds beat me.' There were 175. There were a dozen over 60. And all these Fs! I'd never raced against women before and 110 of them beat me! Including a kid of 15 who shouldn't have been in the race at all, she beat me! I got beaten by two *walkers*!

I couldn't go to my grave as a Cambridge Blue and a Birchfield Harrier, beaten in my first marathon by two walkers. And I started thinking, 'How come all these old guys beat me?' I'd been running 22 miles a week, 9-minute miles. The day after *Running* magazine came out, I started training for my next marathon.

No idea when it could be. But I started going faster. Within a couple of months, I was doing 7-minute miles in my training, because every Sunday morning from September through to April from eleven to half past twelve I was running intervals. It's called refereeing a soccer match. I was belting round, 20 or 30 yards at a time, over a hundred times a match. So that was why I got fitter for racing marathons. I had no idea at the time but it all went down in the training diary and after a couple of years you realise what's been going on.

I used to think racing interrupted training. Now I've got my heart-rate monitor, I've realised that when racing my heart rate is five beats more. When I'm racing 10-minute miles I only need an average heart rate of 135 over eight or nine hours. When I'm doing a short ultra like 50k I run nearer 8-minute miles and sustain nearer 145. When I run a 10k I'm sustaining nearer 160. In order to get your heart to deliver more, you've got to grow it. Grow the muscle. Stress it by training it at a rate higher than you're going to race with it.

Last year from the middle of March to the end of May I ran ten races in twelve weeks. The shortest was 25 miles and the longest was the 100k championships in mid-May. I did the Leeds Marathon, a week after, plus the London Marathon, and several half-marathons and 10ks. And at the end of that I went to South Africa to run in the Comrades Marathon, and the day before my resting heart rate was 34. My haematologist says, 'In my business we get worried if someone's resting heart rate is 44, never mind 34.'

London is the priority this year, not for a time but to finish because it's the 100th. I have to confess that the purists would say it's the 81st, because since I got involved in ultras instead of running five or six marathons a year I've only been running one or two, the rest being ultramarathons. So I've been counting every ultra I've run beyond the marathon distance as one marathon.

The slowest I've ever run in a marathon is 3.49.57, which was my first London. I've only been close to that twice, once when I had a hamstring injury and once because I'd only trained 15 miles a week. I've been past Buckingham Palace eighteen times and I haven't seen it yet. I concentrate on the bottom in front. But I don't care what time I run in. Six hours would do. It doesn't count unless you finish. It doesn't count unless you start, which is why I'm going to be careful about where I race in the next few weeks. I don't want to go belting round the hills, where I could get injured. I shall be devastated if I don't finish.

Jill Demilew was born in Wales in 1955 and now lives in Blackheath with her husband, Yeshiwas, and son Daniel. She is a midwife. She is running the London Marathon in memory of her daughter, Miriam, who died in 1996.

To:
Sarah Kennard,
Marathon Fund-raising Co-ordinator,
Whizz-Kidz

14th December 1998

Dear Sarah,
I had already applied to run in the London Marathon and was intending to raise money for Whizz-Kidz. Unfortunately, I was unsuccessful in the draw. It was a pleasant surprise to read in the booklet that was sent to me that Whizz-Kidz is the official charity this year and may have places available for people who can raise £1,500.

Although I have never run a marathon I have been 'social' jogging for the last ten years with a good friend. She helped to keep me steady and hopeful during the years we had our daughter Miriam with us.

As a family, we and especially Miriam benefited from Whizz-Kidz. You raised the money for her last powered wheelchair. Broomleigh Housing Association in Bromley raised it on a golfing day. Miriam and I visited them to say thank you . . . etc. Miriam also went to the House of Lords to represent Whizz-Kidz and receive a cheque. We also as family and friends joined the Midland Bank 12-mile London Walks on two occasions. Miriam was pushed all 12 miles by her friends Adam and Ben. Miriam was on the first 'user group' of children. For one who had such limited mobility, she certainly got around. One of her last jaunts was with a group of friends in the wheelchair to Brighton for a pop concert (without adults). Great time had by all. Would have been very different without the wheelchair.

I really want the opportunity to give back. I will do my best to raise the £1,500 but am not sure. But to run

is important to me, this once. Please consider me as an option.
I look forward to hearing from you,
Jill.

I used to watch it every year and get overwhelmed with it, the sea of bobbing heads. I was working two nights a week as a midwife at Greenwich Hospital and what my family didn't know (they thought I was safely tucked up in bed) was that I'd nip out of bed and watch it on the telly. And even as an independent midwife, from 1988, I'd say, 'Please let me know if your labour's starting before seven in the morning because if it's marathon day it's going to be harder to get away.' In the latter years we used to go up to the wheelchair start – Yeshiwas my husband and Daniel our son and Miriam when she was alive. She died over two years ago on 31 December. The last day of 1996.

Just after Miriam was born, I said that she was in pain. She had fat thighs and a sort of bracelet on one leg and I shrank from putting her nappy on. On the second day of her life, the junior paediatrician said, 'Let's X-ray her.' The leg was broken in three places – thigh, tib and fib. The sinister part was that they weren't fresh fractures – she'd done that in the womb. I remember being told by an elderly consultant that I'd have to treat her like my grandmother's best china.

I never handled her like a normal baby. Before I factually knew something was wrong, I instinctively knew. I had to change her very slowly on a flat surface, moving her from side to side to minimise the pain, this little bundle of broken bones. When she was three weeks old I picked her up from her carry cot and I knew she was in great pain. I had her at the breast. I remember her crying and knew it wasn't her leg. I hadn't even thought at that time that it could affect anything except her leg.

I took her down to casualty and it was grim and horrible.

We didn't have a car. I remember walking down the road with my baby in midsummer in a shawl. I finally got seen after five hours, at midnight. She had a broken arm.

I knew it was serious but I still didn't know what was serious. We went to Great Ormond Street for the definitive diagnosis, and because of a dispute with the clerks, nobody would go and get her results. It was a hellish time. I didn't have a clue about brittle bone disease. The correct name is osteogenesis imperfecta – the imperfect making of bones. It's a collagen disorder. You get a very warped skeleton. Your long bones don't grow. It's obvious, it's in your face; you've got a deformity. Everyone else grew and she didn't.

Finally, a friend passed on my name to the Society for Brittle Bone Disease and this heavenly woman rang and 24 hours later we had a box of goodies: ordinary baby clothes which had been split down the middle and had Velcro sewn in. A woolly elephant, the sort your grandma might make. He was grey with a little red waistcoat; that was for Daniel. Then a rattle that someone had put a layer of cotton wool round so if Daniel bashed her it wouldn't hurt. I remember weeping over that.

When I look back on it, I think there was a lot of existing going on. But we had wonderful friends. Jen, my great running mate, she lives just along the triangle of roads here. I used to go past her pregnant with Miriam and she'd see me getting bigger and bigger and shouting at Dan not to wee in the manholes. I used to have Miriam in a great big carriage pram, because of the suspension. Jen peered in and said, 'Pop in for coffee one day.' I was so vulnerable, tears always welling up. I went to Jen's and just burst into tears on the threshold, and a great friendship began that day.

Jen, bless her. We wept together. Her second daughter, Nancy, had developed severe epilepsy out of the blue, so she was no stranger to pain about kids. She's run regularly for years, whereas over that time I've probably run for a few months with her then left it for a couple of years, then gone back to it. At times, I couldn't run up to the main road and back again without being puffed. She started me running, she carried me on – and she's probably going to finish me off! She's one of life's encouragers. I now realise how important running is to her. It's how she lived through what it was like with Nancy. I delivered her third baby, when she was 40. Tom. He's 10 now.

With Miriam, from nought to three was just hard. Plod, plod, plod. Existing. I'm not saying there weren't joyful times but it was hard. Miriam always had open eyes, staring at you, drinking the world in. Daniel was at Robert Owen nursery school and the deputy head, Mary Tinker, said, 'Are you thinking of bringing Miriam here?' I owe a lot to her.

It was around the start of integrated education, we were at the very beginning. I had to be on the premises every day. Miriam had this dinky old chair, electric, that she called Zippy Red. She'd always been carried, she couldn't independently move, she couldn't even bottom shuffle, but she was a very powerful person. She could shout and scream. But unlike Dan, she wouldn't be a great enthusiast; she'd reserve her judgement. But she got into Zippy Red and mastered a three-point turn in five minutes. In Zippy Red she was a bugger. In the playground there was a slope for go-karts. All the boys and the girls would go down it and Miriam decided to play this game; she'd go across in Zippy Red as they went down. This little thing. This little person.

It was a fight to get her into mainstream education. The first school we tried, where our vicar's daughter went, we weren't even allowed to look round. Fear, I suppose. I look back on that period of my life and think, 'How did we survive?' I began to get a bit politicised then. I was beginning to wise up. We ended up in a wonderful four-storey Victorian school with no lift where the head said, 'Every child is special,' and in she went, with a carer, went through that primary school. It was great. The school caretaker made a ramp for her himself, and changed the girls' ground-floor loos. She had a chair on the top floor and a chair on the bottom, and at weekly fire drill the caretaker would carry her down and she'd twiddle his moustache on the way.

When Jen and I are running we talk about the peaks of life. Jen was really, really grieved at Miriam's death. We talk about that last summer of Miriam's life. She was on the crest of a wave that year. She went to pop concerts. She had sleepovers with friends. But one night that summer she woke up in the middle of the night with the horrors. About death and dying. She said to me, 'How do I know God's there?'

I said, 'That'll be your journey.'

She said, 'I don't want people to be sad.' It was a great last year. But I remember that night when it was fear.

Her death was a real shock. The only thing that I was aware of was that if we'd had a car crash or anything and needed resuscitation it couldn't have been done for Miriam. She still had a major break a year but she wasn't so fragile. I had seen adults with that degree of brittle bone disease. I knew it was life-limiting but I suppose I'd said to myself, 'She'll make 60.' She was a healthy child. I remember her being physically sick only once in her life.

A couple of summers before she died, she took part in *Look Who's Talking* for Channel 4 Children's Week. Eleven-to-fourteen-year-olds talking about what they thought would make a better Britain. So she had chances and opportunities. Whizz-Kidz decided to have a User Board and Miriam was one of the first members. She did two 12-mile walks for them, with her friends Ben and Adam pushing her around. So she was an ambassador for Whizz-Kidz. And as part of the TV and video she did, she got to talk to ministers for the disabled.

She learned to play the piccolo when she was 12. The

squeaky piccolo. She had to learn the fife first, to improve her lung function. She really loved it and she eventually played a solo at the school concert. She was at the John Roan school by then, with Dan. She sang in the choir. In 1997, the school made a trip to a kraal in Guyana. They sang Adiemos. She was going to go. She never made it.

She was $14\frac{1}{2}$ when she died. Usually we had Christmas at my parents' in Wales and I'd be back to work New Year's Eve but this particular year, I said, 'I've got to do my turn,' and Yesh and I agreed we'd have Christmas here and New Year in Wales. Dan got flu, Yesh got it and Miriam and I were fine. I played the organ at our church, St Nick's in Deptford, and then we went to Christmas lunch with a great friend. The sick boys got up for it. It was a very happy evening. We played games. The day after Boxing Day, she wasn't well. But she seemed to be getting over it: a 99-degree temperature, but she wanted to go to Grandma's and it was down by midday.

By the time we got to Wales she was breathing fast. We rang and got a rota GP, a nice bloke who said, 'Yep, got a chest infection, here's a prescription for antibiotics and if you're worried, call me back.' We weren't worried. She wasn't chesty, wasn't asthma-y, she just broke her bones.

The next day we went to Boots and got her a vaporiser. On New Year's Eve, I knew she was poorly. I bathed her and dried her and helped her eat, which wasn't her style. We put her to bed at eight. Mum and Dad went to bed. Dan was out. At midnight Yesh went to check on her and she was cold. In my bed. My childhood bed. She must have been dead for a few hours.

I remember touching her and thinking, 'She's not there.' She just looked asleep, very peaceful. I said to Yesh, 'We're going to have to get Dan home. You cannot be scared of death. It would be utterly cruel to leave him overnight.'

Dan was utterly devastated that she died. He just didn't

think she could ever die. She was as invincible as anyone else. He'd never seen her potential frailty as I had – the last two years when adult organs were trying to creep into a tiny frame. But it's just not something you expect.

A horrid doctor came. The police came. The inspector remembered Dad from when he was a lad and used to go to the Christian coffee bar. They were great, but they interviewed Yesh and I separately, like a cot death. I was horrified they could think of a post mortem. I said, 'No. We know why she died.' I was distraught at the idea that they could cut up my daughter's body.

Because she was cold when I touched her I knew that she had died on the 31st of December, not the 1st of January. That was the only thing that mattered for me. I was glad that she'd died at the end of the year, not the beginning. She's got a simple headstone, with her name and the dates and, 'She was a happy girl.'

I'm training with Jen, Sarah and Ros. It used to be, 'If only . . .' or, 'Why shouldn't we?' When we jogged around the park, it was, 'Maybe.' Then when Jen hit 50, she said, 'It's now or never.' Sometime last summer after a run. 'Let's do it, why not?'

I don't think any of us realised the commitment. We put our names in the draw and then I broke my arm rushing to get to church, slipping on a flagstone. I was playing the organ and I got up to reach the organ stops and thought, 'God, my arm's stiff.' I tried to pull my knickers up in the loo, and when my friend heard me say, 'Oo,' she said, 'You're going to casualty.' So that was me off training till December and then I was the only one of us four who didn't get a place.

I was terribly, terribly grieved when I couldn't get in. I wrote to Whizz-Kidz. I'd learned that I'd have to raise £1,500 and I didn't know if I could, working in the NHS. So

I wrote in with a heartfelt plea and a story of why I needed to run. And I really needed to run by then. And they said yes, I could have a place anyway.

Jen is running for the National Epilepsy Society, Ros for Neville's Runners and Sarah for Breakthrough because she had breast cancer two years ago. You become very close when you train together. Your emotional lives become intertwined. We ran to Charing Cross recently, by the river. Piddling down with rain. One of the things that will stay with me for the rest of my life is that I'm a very social runner, and it's a bit like the confessional. This is the place where you can say anything, and I've been saying, 'I *hate* running but I do love my friends.'

Samuel 'Joe' Fell was born in Ireland in 1944 and now lives in Bromley, Kent. He became a runner at the age of 48 having spent most of his adult life as an alcoholic. He belongs to Dulwich Runners and, racing as a veteran, has won many individual and county medals. This is his sixth London Marathon. He runs under the name of Samuel in honour of his grandfather; his friends know him as Joe.

Joe Fell's training log
    Week 12.
    Mon. DONE (10) miles. Speed 9 × 600 metres. Got to Foxgrove Road Min38–Sec48 got to Bell Green Min18–Sec20. (fit)
    Tue. DONE (10) miles. Trail. (hard) Time 69.35 Grove Park, (PARK), up THEATRE. Felt tired but strong. OK. HARD.
    Wed. A.M. DONE (8) miles. Fast to hard. Feel fit. Power. P.M. DONE (6) miles (3) power.
    Thur. Had a rest. Chest cold.
    Fri. DONE. (8) miles. Some speed. Still got chest

cold. Foxgrove Road. Time 32.40 and that was easy to steady.

Sat. Went to France. Had a rest.

Sun. DONE (15) miles. ($\frac{1}{2}$ marathon). Race time 1.29.11. First (50) in the club championships.

I've always been a competitive bloke. Even if you're a dustman, be the best dustman in the world. I had to be the best alcoholic, the best streetfighter, the best at eating the most free dinners from the rubbish bins behind Tesco.

I started drinking when I was 23. I was a boxer for many years: amateur, but I was reasonably good at it. Then my marriage broke up: I married very young. Then I took to drink. Within two years I was an alcoholic. I was homeless for 20-odd years. I used to live in the city. I slept on park benches. Brixton was my manor.

Alcohol was with me 24 hours a day. Five o'clock in the morning, I'd start. A lot of us were like that. Most of my friends are dead now. I got very seriously ill and I often felt suicidal. I just couldn't live with myself any more.

And then one day I met a policeman. Because I was asleep on the street, drunk. I wanted to stop and he said, 'If you want to stop, you'll stop, but there's no easy way.' He was a recovered alcoholic himself. He sent me down to the Salvation Army in Whitechapel and I got detoxed. Six weeks it took, because I was so bad; usually it takes ten days.

After the six weeks, they placed me in the Alcohol Recovery Project in Camberwell. That was very difficult. Counselling for three months. Very heavy. Around a big table. Seven women and two men. Sometimes the women are more messed up than the men. It was very difficult to talk in front of all these people, but I talked. Get it all out, don't bottle it up.

My life story is that I never grew mentally from 23 to 44. I didn't know who the Prime Minister was when I woke up

THE RUNNERS

from that existence. I never had a council flat. I never had my own room. I was a kind of lone alcoholic. People sensed something in me. I think I frightened them a bit. I had a reputation for being a bit aggressive. I think I did it on purpose. You lived in an environment where physical violence happened every day. I was the man with blood running down his face and drinking from a bottle at the same time.

I wanted recognition. It's the low esteem. From the way my dad treated me. I don't think he understood that kids need a little bit of praise. I ran away from home when I was 15. I was more frightened of my dad than I was of sleeping in a field.

He wanted me to be a farmer. I couldn't see myself as that. And I rebelled against the organised religion. I got sickened over the years. I went into a church once when I was drunk and stood up at the back and shouted, 'You're a fucking bollix.' There must have been something about the church for me to go into it and attack the priest. Paranoia sets in. It was a compulsion. The same as I had when I saw all those brolly blokes going to work. I'd be sitting on my park bench and I'd say, 'Your wife's at home with the milkman now.' I was jealous, I suppose.

I'll have been dry ten years this September. A great man sorted me out. I was dry six days. Then six more days. Then . . . for ever, ever, ever. It cracks you up. Giving up fags was nothing; nothing was as hard as giving up drink.

I was 44 when I stopped drinking and I came out nearly 22 months later when I was 46. I sat here for about two years doing nothing. I painted the flat. I have a friend and I painted her flat. All these things to keep me occupied so I wasn't taking a little drink. I thought, 'I'll give up smoking. That'll give me something to do.' I stopped smoking. I got on the scales one day and I was $14\frac{1}{2}$ stone because I hadn't been doing anything. I've always been a bit of an athlete: not a brains person, more the physical type, so I thought, 'I'll have a little jog.'

Well, you can imagine. Alcohol had left me with a lot of problems, including peripheral neuritis in my legs. It's the nerve endings: it goes to the calves, then the hands and then the head, when it's called wet brain. Dementia. It was up to my calves and I used to get it so bad I couldn't walk.

But after about a year jogging I decided I'd enter a race. My legs had started to get better. I wasn't getting these bad hips any more. My first race ever was a 10k at Crystal Palace. I bought a pair of shorts, I put them on and I ran 44 minutes. Not bad! I went into the library and got out a book about running. Three months later I did a 10k at Herne Hill in 40.07.

I tried to get into the London Marathon but they refused me. But I kept training and I started getting faster. I went to Stockholm to meet my son; he's 32, lives in Sweden, just doing his Masters Doctorate in Politics at the moment. I ran Stockholm in 3.21 and he did 3.53. The battle between him and me has gone on for a few years. He'd ring me to say he'd done 3.30; I'd have done 3.18. Then he rang one day and said, 'I've done 3.20.' Then I wrote and said I'd done 3.06. So I'm still in the lead. So far.

My first London was in 1994. I did 3.18.31, but I was still fat then. In 1997 I did 3.06.20; I got my weight down to ten stone and it meant twelve minutes to me. A pound in a marathon is a minute. Lose ten pounds and you'll be ten minutes faster. Except if you're a woman. It isn't the same with a woman. Then it's lose ten pounds and you'll be twenty minutes faster.

I get an automatic place in the marathon because I'm fast for my age. I'll be on Green Start with the footballers. I'm averaging around 60 miles a week. I have one day off a week completely, sometimes two if I'm very tired, because if you don't rest you'll put tiredness on top of tiredness. My long

Sunday run has been around 22 miles. I'll do two 25s, one of them six weeks before London, the other one four weeks before. I'll run those at marathon pace. Then after the second I'll know if I'm ready or not. Then I'll wind down.

I've done everything in my life. Barman, bouncer, painter and decorator. When I stopped drinking, I found out I was quite good at a lot of things. When you're an alcoholic, you're just looking for the wage packet. You don't care if you lay a floor upside down. Very greedy people, alcoholics. Go into a bar, you see the lines of people part. You're smelly, your clothes are bad, you've no money. You're begging. The things you do to get money.

I have a good life now. I go swimming. I ride my mountain bike. I do a bit of gardening for people. I love running. I laugh and joke but underneath all that is a very serious runner. Before a race I will look to see which other 50-year-olds are in it. There's an obsessive aspect to running. It can take over, rule your life a bit. Alcoholics are that way anyway – obsessive. You have to be careful. I take three weeks off a year. Lose all my fitness and have to start again. Otherwise my body would break down because I'd just run and run. My partner says to me, 'Joe, why do you have to win all the time?' It's the way I was made.

Gail Nerurkar was born in 1965 in Heidelberg where her father was working in the physics department of the university. The family returned to England shortly afterwards and she grew up with her sister and two brothers in Oxfordshire. She runs for Thames Hare and Hounds and is married to the British international marathoner Richard Nerurkar. She is an epidemiologist and GP, and lives in Teddington, south-west London. This is her first marathon.

Runner's World Training Log

  Week beginning 4/1.

  M. a.m. Distance 10k. Time 45.19. To Park (Ham Gate – Kingston Gate) – riverside. p.m. Distance 4k. To cycle shop in Kingston.

  T. a.m. Distance 7k. Time 34. Around Marlborough with Sue Tulloh and Helen Stokes. p.m. Distance 11k. Time 46.30. Missed track. Kingston flooded. Traffic jam. 11k road loop. Stormed it because so annoyed.

  W. a.m. Distance 5k. Time 22. Easy round Lensbury. p.m. Distance 14k. Time 80. Horrible evening but did track session inc. 4×4 mins with $1\frac{3}{4}$ mins recovery round a road loop with Rachel Disley. Better runner than me so I'm chasing her. Richard leaving for S.A. so had supper with her.

  Th. Distance 10k. Time 46.

  Riverside – Home Park – Bushy Park.

  F. Distance 7k. Time 34. Inc. strides, in Bushy Park.

  Sat. a.m. Distance 4+k. Time 19. Easy at Lensbury. p.m. Surrey League cross-country (Richmond Park) – 5k – 12th in 22.50. Rachel 2nd in 20.11.

  Sun. Distance 20k. Time 94. a.m. around Esher/Claygate/Thames Ditton with Rachel and Alison Carpenter.

  Weekly Total 103k.

  Total year to date 175k.

I trained as a doctor; I qualified in 1990. I did four years in hospital medicine, three years' research at the School of Hygiene and Tropical Diseases, had a little bit of time abroad and a little bit in general practice. Now I work at St George's Hospital four days a week and do a half day as a GP. I love a mixture like that. Some research, some teaching, some hands-on. It's great. Really good.

  I spent a lot of my childhood doing gymnastics; I was

training from 8 to 15 and got to national level. But then I began to feel I was getting pretty stiff, I couldn't do all the bending I used to do, and anyway I thought I'd better put something into my A levels. I suppose the biggest things that happened around that time was that I became a Christian in my last year at school and that influenced what I did in my gap year; I went to help out in a church on the outskirts of Birmingham. I stayed with the vicar and his family. The experience was pretty important for the medicine later on. I had a great time.

I went to Pembroke College, Cambridge, where I was in the first intake of girls. Among other things, I started rowing a lot. I was on the verge of the university lightweight boat. I was cut out on the final cut, which at the time was a major disappointment.

Then I did my clinical training in Whitechapel and lived in Bethnal Green. It was harder to do team sports by then, particularly as you slowly take on bits of responsibility as a medical student. I went to a few cross-country races simply because I thought that was a way of getting on a bus and going somewhere nicer for an afternoon.

Through that I ended up going on a London University team in 1989 to run an *ekiden* – which is Japanese for relay race – in Osaka, so I suppose I must have been reasonably good as a runner, but I hadn't really grasped the idea of systematic training and how you can get better by it. For the London Hospital Children's Unit I got sponsored to run the 1989 Paris Marathon but that was very much a 'Let's jog round with some other medical students' type of thing. So I laboured round in about four hours. It wasn't desperately pleasant; it was hard work. A beautiful route but cobble-stones when you didn't want any.

I became a houseman and time for most other activities was minimal. It was a state of survival for two or three years. I moved up to Sheffield. It was hilly. You could cycle out and be in the Peaks in 20 minutes, and I was occasionally, pretty sporadically running even then, but I think the long months of what is chronic sleep deprivation are not good for anybody and weren't particularly good for me. But during those three years I had a short time in Zimbabwe, in the south-west, out in the bush. I was clinical officer in a tiny hospital run by the Salvation Army.

I suppose that was part of a process of involvement with medicine in various forms in Africa. I had the very strong sense that we were always fire-fighting instead of preventing problems before they happened. So I was looking for a more public health/research slant to my work and that's when the job came up at the London School of Hygiene.

I went there in 1994, for three years, and ran two projects. One was a community survey in Madras, looking at whether there is a familial tendency to accumulate fat in the stomach area rather than the hips: apple rather than pear. In September 1994 I sent out 2,000 letters to men inviting them to take part in my study and Richard was the recipient of one of them.

I'd met him at a mutual friend's wedding and I simply thought it would be great to have him involved in the project as an Anglo-Indian. I guess things just went from there. He did help out with the project and we started seeing each other, and in 1996, after the Atlanta Olympics, we got married and moved here.

I suppose my running was sparked off enormously because it was great to try and share that part of Richard's life, particularly because it's jolly cold watching cross-country races rather than doing it yourself. I started systematic training in 1995, when I was 29.

My training is variable. I can commute by running: an easy/steady run of $8\frac{1}{2}$ miles into work. It takes just over an hour. I've got a tiny thing on my wrist with my keys and money in it, and it ensures I don't take work home. I keep clothes in my filing cabinet.

That's twice a week. I do a track session on Tuesdays in Kingston; there's always a group of girls and veteran men who are doing things around my pace. Once a week I do a long run. One and a half hours, which will go up to three hours as the marathon gets nearer.

I love it. I suppose it brings a whole range of new challenges, whether it's just completing a good session, running a good race or doing three hours for the first time. Just being outside in the fresh air is great and it's time to think about things. I'm quite often writing something. I'll have thoughts going around my head and when I get back they're clear. You just feel great as well: the waking-up effect, the euphoria.

About six months ago I thought I'd love to have a try at the marathon but the furthest I'd run till then had been ten miles. So I tested myself out by doing some half-marathons over the summer. I have to say I didn't definitely decide to do London till I knew what Richard was going to do, because we weren't sure we could both train for it and support each other adequately. Particularly as in the lead-up to a marathon it's important to Richard that he can rest. And I do sports massage on him and if I'm knackered as well it might not have a good effect, and this is his living.

Richard's slight loss of form at the beginning of this year made it clearer. It didn't affect him if I decided to run. It was fractional. He was 99.5 per cent and that's not enough. He decided that unless he was fully fit he shouldn't run and his training suggested he wasn't on top form.

It's a strange feeling that I'm preparing for this big race, beginning to focus psychologically on it as well, and Richard is looking after *me*. I don't think I feel guilty, but it is slightly odd. It means that if I go to a track session he will get some supper ready when I get back, and after a Sunday long run he'll get the bath running.

I'm hoping to do around three hours, which will get me onto the elite. But a three-hour goal is like a 3.30 or a 4.00: a bit of a magic number. Three hours is a goal that seems not entirely realistic. A second goal would be 3.05 and a tertiary goal will be getting round intact.

Antony Read was born in 1957. A computer systems operator, he lives in Redhill, Surrey, with his wife Jo and sons Stuart and Ben. After completing his first marathon at 17 in a time of 3.25, he went on the next year to run his second in 3.05. As well as running for Redhill and Surrey Beagles, he is also a keen motorcycle trialist. In August 1980, after a hit-and-run driver knocked him off his motorbike, his right leg had to be amputated below the knee.

JANUARY
Sun 3. Race (Epsom 10) 82.05. Up and downhill all the way
Tue 5. 11½ miles mountain bike
Wed 6. Run 5 miles
Fri 8. 17 miles mountain bike
Sun 10. Run 11 miles

It's strange, I thought I'd lost the leg straight away. To this day I'm not sure why, but when I got knocked off the bike I looked down and saw both bones broken and the leg twisted round and I thought it was clean off.

At that instant I knew I was in a bad way and I needed help quickly. It was ten to eleven; I was on my way to do nightshift at work. I slid along the ground and ended up in a pub car park, and I screamed for help; I was bleeding badly. It must be a self-preservation thing. In theory I probably should have passed out but it wasn't till I got to hospital that I relaxed. I can't remember the pain but it was intense. I said, 'Knock me out.'

The accident happened on the Wednesday, my new motorbike was due to be delivered on the Friday and I was having my birthday party on the Saturday night, so that all went out the window. I was three months in hospital. The front of the leg was totally wiped away. They couldn't plate it, they couldn't pin it. There was this new thing on the market called electrobiology. You have your leg in plaster and two pads that you put on either side at night. They plug you into the mains for twelve hours and it sends magnetic pulses through the bone. That's to try and stimulate the bone to grow, but it didn't work for me.

It sounds difficult, but in reality it wasn't. It was almost more difficult for those around me. When you're injured you know exactly what's going on but the others around you view it differently. I was so active prior to the accident, the sort of person who's hardly ever sitting down and always used to being around people, and now I was stuck in hospital, flat on my back, all on my own. People thought, 'Will he be able to cope?'

Before the accident Jo and I had bought a house which I'd been living in on my own. Jo was still living with her parents and working up in London. So when I came out of hospital after three months, Jo got a transfer to Horley. Otherwise I would have had to go back to my parents.

After another three months I went back to hospital to find out whether the treatment was working. I was readmitted straight away. Although the wound had healed, the break was exactly the same and it was like the last six months had achieved nothing.

I didn't like the thought of going back in again. I couldn't look forward, I couldn't plan my future, I didn't know what state I'd be in, whether I'd have a leg I could walk on, no leg or whatever. The consultant came round on the Tuesday and we had a very heavy discussion. All through my dealings with him he'd mentioned that there was no guarantee of saving the leg, but it was me who raised the subject of amputation. He said, 'Give me a week to weigh up all the options and unless I can come back with 90 per cent certainty that you'll have a working leg in six months' time, we'll amputate.'

There wasn't any grief. You want to get on with your life. Being a below-the-knee amputee is a major difference to above. Even then I felt confident that if I lost the leg I was still going to get on and do things. I had an elderly uncle who lost one leg above the knee and one below through diabetes, and he learnt to walk again with crutches in his 70s, and I thought, 'If he can learn that at his age then I can run again.'

So when the consultant came back I was more afraid he was going to say, 'Let's try this, that or the other,' than, 'Let's amputate.' I got married on crutches. I actually made a cardboard leg for that because the trousers wouldn't hang right. There was no way I was going to get married in a wheelchair.

It was always my desire to run again, but it was a slow process. My big ambition was to run the London Marathon but every time I tried regularly to run more than three miles daily something would go wrong and my stump would break down. Over the next few years we kept trying out and modifying the legs but the stump kept breaking down; I'd have to stop running for a few weeks and then start over again. I'd set myself a target of running the marathon by the age of 35 and I figured if I hadn't achieved it by then, I never would. So effectively I spent ten years chasing a dream, and failed.

I continued running to keep fit and it did mean I was a very active amputee; I competed in motorcycle trials, played football and went skiing every other year. But by the time I was 37, running just two miles a day was giving serious problems and though Roehampton Limb Centre tried to resolve them by making me a new leg I had to give up altogether. So I started going to the gym and cycling to keep fit.

Then I heard about Chris Moon, who was going to attempt the London Marathon eighteen months after he lost his leg. One, he was attempting to do what I'd failed to do, and two, he was doing it within only eighteen months. This was at the stage I'd been forced to give up running. Up pops this young upstart and the bugger goes out and does what I'd always wanted to do. I wanted to find out what he'd got.

I've always found at Roehampton that I've never had a problem getting the hardware. If you feel you warrant having a better leg, they give it to you. Chris Moon was using a new leg called a VSP and my doctor at Roehampton agreed for me to have one. It's got a piston, and a spring which the foot is fixed onto. That is what enables me to run. So Chris Moon got there first but I was determined to go faster.

I built up to regular 6-mile runs and on 5 October 1998 I entered a 10k race in Battersea Park. I'd set out to break 50 minutes; 8-minute miling, $3\frac{1}{2}$ laps of Battersea Park. My son Stuart was calling out times off his watch as I came round and when I came round for my third lap I misheard and thought I was a minute slower than I was, so I hurried up and actually got in in 48.55, 220 out of 391.

It was time to get my marathon entry organised. Although I'd started to feel good, my intention had been to get my own place and not go public till February when I'd be more confident of achieving what I wanted, so I applied through the normal channels and was as gutted as anybody to be rejected.

I got the rejection on the Friday. I went through *Runner's World* looking at all the different options. I've never had a favourite charity but I wanted something to do with what I had, especially with disabled kids. I got up Saturday morning and said, 'Right, I'm going for Whizz-Kidz,' because I liked the way they were coming across. I found they'd got places left, told them about myself and arranged to go up and see them. I had to raise £1,500. So I went to see my boss at Monotype and he said, 'We'll definitely put up £750 but I can't commit to any more till I've talked to some other people,' and then after five minutes he said, 'Oh stuff it, we'll put up the £1,500.'

Around the time of the Battersca Park 10k I was starting to get into a conventional training pattern, but about a week after that the stump broke down, probably because I'd pushed too hard too soon. So I've taken the decision that I'm not going to run too often but that I'm going to use a bike for half my training. Everything you read says if you only run twice a week you don't improve, but I'm hoping to prove them wrong.

The Race

The Skin-and-Bone Men

Long before I became a runner, I had two ancient and somewhat tenuous connections with the London Marathon. The first was that after I got married in the early 1980s, we moved to a house just off Greenwich Park. Thus it was that without having to do anything more athletically demanding than stroll to the top of the road one Sunday morning we could witness the start of the biggest mass-participation sporting event in the British Isles. The London Marathon was not as humungous a spectacle as it is now, but nevertheless having nearly 8,000 people in shorts thunder past your back yard was not something you forgot in a hurry.

When we had seen off everyone from the world's elite to the people aiming to toss pancakes all the way to Westminster Bridge we could drift down to the *Cutty Sark* and see the same river of humanity, not quite as *soigné* now they were more than six miles into the task but still an inspirationally joyous mob. Like most people watching on the sidelines in those days, it never occurred to me that I might one day be in there with elbows flying and a marinade of Vaseline and talcum powder squelching around inside my trainers. Then I believed that only exceptionally gifted athletes or the borderline loony would take on a 26.2.

Even at that stage of the game, competing in a marathon was to the majority of British citizens the ultimate act either of athletic courage or eccentric folly. Growing up in the late 1950s and then through the 1960s I had been fascinated, though more by its potential for human drama than out of sportswriterly appreciation. Jim Peters – he *collapsed*! Sergey Popov was a *Russian*! (In that era Russians were mysterious and sinister; they spied, built Sputniks and were in all likelihood going to blow us all up.)

Then Abebe Bikila ran through Rome, as light and sere as a twig. He was an Ethiopian, the first black African Olympic marathon champion, and he ran barefoot. Hooked, I tuned into every Olympics thereafter on the family's black-and-white TV set, to wonder and (I have to confess) watch with grisly relish those skin-and-bone men broken by heat, pace and distance, staggering bent and dehydrated, with legs like pipe cleaners and lolling heads, to the finishing tape in some exotically distant stadium.

I make jokes about running marathons because the way I run them reveals a comic gap between aspiration and experience. I know, though, that to win one involves the demonstration of superhuman gifts of fleetness, stamina, grit and mental toughness. I was born too late to be thrilled first-hand by the feats of Emil Zatopek in the 1952 Olympics in Helsinki, but twenty years on I was to read about them in a column by Red Smith, the greatest of American sports writers. It told me all I needed to know about what long-distance running takes at the rarefied end of the business:

> The world now knows that Emil Zatopek, the Czech nobody can pass, won the Olympic marathon after winning at 5,000 and 10,000 meters. No man, or other animal, or foot-racer, or masochist, ever contemplated such a triple before, and none will again until they start recruiting track teams from the booby hatch. Zatopek

used to be a messenger boy, and there's a helluva future for him with Western Union should he attempt a comeback.

There were also marathons being staged in Britain throughout these years, of course. It was just that hardly anyone outside the athletics world took notice, or because they were unofficial, even solipsistic affairs, run by enthusiasts in rural privacy, out of bloody-mindedness or curiosity, to see if they could go 26 miles and come away alive.

There had even been a marathon in the capital before, during the London Olympics of 1908. Johnny Hayes of the USA took gold in 2.55.19, a time which these days is within the scope of hundreds of the best club runners, but then must have seemed a miracle of fortitudinous endurance. An Italian, Dorando Pietro, fell to bits just before the finish but came back the following year for more, pitting himself against the Brit D. W. Gardener on a track of coconut matting in the Albert Hall. For the record, Gardener won. There was no agonising then in the sports pages about the disappointing state of British long-distance running.

But even in the Britain of the 1970s, even though what the Americans called jogging had dragged a few plump, wheezy blobs off their sofas and into whittled, evangelical and usually fleeting firmness, simply taking part in a 26.2 for no other reason than because it was there seemed an activity that on the Richter scale of self-punishing nuttiness ranked alongside walking on live coals or chucking out your mattress in favour of a bed of broken glass. That the Americans went in for it was yet another example of excessive, populous, across-the-pond unhingement. Yes, throwing open the bridges and avenues of New York for the day to thousands of ordinary men, women and children wearing vests, shorts, waiter's outfits, fur, whiskers, hide, funny ears and *papier mâché* constructs of clocks and national monuments was just the sort of thing they'd get up to over there. But over here? For that we have to thank, among others, the man who represents my other tenuous connection with the London Marathon.

Years before, when I was an underling of almost majestic incompetence and fecklessness on the *Observer* sports desk, one of the reporters whose press passes I regularly mislaid and whose flights home I criminally forgot to book was a man called Chris Brasher.

To someone in whose mental stockpile of Great Moments in Sport was the image of a stocky, grimacing, physically punished but undaunted young Englishman battling his way to an Olympic steeplechase gold medal in Melbourne in 1956, Chris Brasher was not the middle-aged athletics correspondent of a Sunday broadsheet but a figure of God-like power and fortitude (albeit one who by then smoked a particularly infernal pipe).

I recalled that in winning his medal Brasher had survived a move to disqualify him for barging and although I never experienced the man as anything less than genial, there was a forceful and direct quality about him which suggested he had been wise not to opt for a career in diplomacy. In fact at the beginning of the 1980s, when I heard that he was planning to bring a marathon, New York style, to this country, I felt not just a stirring of journalistic excitement but a mild concern for anyone who tried to stand in his way.

By then, Brasher had already walked the walk himself. Late in 1979, with Nicholas Luard, the one-time founder of *Private Eye*, he had headed off to run New York. It was an epiphany. Writing eulogistically in the *Observer* on his return of the sights and scenes and crowd support afforded by what he described as 'the greatest folk festival the world has seen', Brasher ended his article by asking whether London could stage such an event:

We have the course, a magnificent course, starting in The Mall and going clockwise around the sights of London and across Tower Bridge and back past St Paul's and into Trafalgar Square, under Admiralty Arch to finish in front of the Palace. But do we have the heart and hospitality to welcome the world?

The answer is that we did, but only through Brasher's persistence. The event has become so much part of national life, the expression 'running the London Marathon' so instantly recognisable as verbal shorthand for everything that is brave and daft and obsessed and noble about the aspiration of ordinary humans to do something uncommon, to rise to the challenge of what Brasher called 'a pointless but wonderful victory over mental doubt and bodily frailty', that it's hard to imagine now the sheer risky, untried novelty of such an idea in 1980.

In fact, however moving and seductive the prospect might have been of a 26-mile, 385-yard road race through the streets of the capital, open to everyone of all ages, backgrounds and genders, from runners at the sharp end who could cover each mile in under five minutes to those who could barely bend over to lace up their trainers, the suspicion is that without Brasher and his co-founder, John Disley, to chivvy the authorities, marshal the great and the good, churn out feasibility plans and hack through thickets of bureaucracy, the project would have suffered the sentence imposed on many great and imaginative ideas: i.e., let it hang around for a while and it won't happen. I thank them both.

The Sharp End: The London Marathon from 1981 to 1998

There is an image which I took away from that first London Marathon which still resonates: the sight of an American and a Norwegian crossing the line together, holding hands in a spontaneous and mutually agreed dead heat. At the time I was moved to hideously embarrassing tears. I saw Dick Beardsley and Inge Simonsen as having run so far together for so long, down such a hard road, that when they reached its end they preferred to recognise and celebrate each other rather than be divided by the aggression needed to choose victory. And it's hard to talk about it now without sounding soppy, but in that gesture of what today would be regarded as almost deranged Corinthianism, they demonstrated everything that is meaningful and human about the marathon.

That inaugural race took place on 29 March 1981. Even in its first year, it was over-subscribed. Some 20,000 hopefuls applied for 7,000 places, an elastic figure, as it turned out: 7,747 runners eventually set out from the start line, of whom 6,253 managed to make it through the rain-swept finish on Constitution Hill behind Beardsley and Simonsen. Their winning time was 2.11.48. Joyce Smith broke the British record to win the women's race in 2.29.57. Smith, the mother of two young daughters, was already 43 years old. I liked that, the revelation that you didn't have to be a babe to break records, that a woman could still wear the crown past 40.

Smith won it again the following year, with a time of 2.29.43 and another UK best. There were more than six minutes between her and the runner-up, New Zealander Lorraine Moller. (And it's extraordinary, the longevity of running life enjoyed by women who do marathons, because a decade later in 1992 Moller was still a top gun, taking bronze in Barcelona.)

That year, 1982, the men's race also went to a Brit. Hugh Jones led from start to finish to beat his PB by 77 seconds, with a 2.09.24 that was the fastest then ever seen in the UK and enough to put him on the world all-time list. The finish was on Westminster Bridge that year, where it stayed till 1994.

What days those were for British long-distance running. Its 15,758 finishers made the 1982 London Marathon the biggest in the world, ahead of New York, whose race director Fred Lebow was among the runners. The class of its field was demonstrated by the fact that 198 people finished inside 2.30. And in 1983, yet another Brit took top honours. Mike Gratton, running in shoulder-to-shoulder rhythm at the front with his countryman Gerry Helme for the best part of the race, opened up a growing and irreducible lead from the Tower of London onwards. He won in 2.09.43. Helme's pre-race PB had been 2.24.51; now he chased Gratton home to clock 2.10.12.

That year, too, saw the London debut of Grete Waitz, the finest woman marathoner in the world. Winning the women's race easily, she set a world best of 2.25.29, though she had less than 24 hours in which to savour her record. Joan Benoit hammered it in Boston the following day.

The Olympics were in Los Angeles in 1984 and the London Marathon was the trial. Gateshead – and Britain again – took the honours thanks to Charlie Spedding who, with his clubmate Kevin Forster, reeled in the wilting leaders, Juma Ikangaa and Zakaria Barie from Tanzania, after 16 miles of scorching pace. Spedding's lonely run to a 2.09.57 finish – he passed the women's race leader Ingrid Kristiansen at 20 miles – earned him his second marathon win in two attempts. Forster was second, just over a minute behind, and Spedding went on to take bronze in Los Angeles. Kristiansen's victory in 2.24.26 was a European record. Priscilla Welch was second.

The London 85 men's race was a duel in the sun. Steve Jones, who had won the Chicago 1984 marathon in a world best 2.08.05, lined up on Blackheath as favourite, but he had

Charlie Spedding to beat. The leading pack reduced gradually as the race wore on. At 15 miles there were six, by 20 there were just Jones and Spedding. At the Tower of London Jones was forced to make a pit stop for stomach cramps. Spedding made a break for it. He'd thought it was a decisive one but suddenly Jones was on his shoulder, then past him. Jones's winning time of 2.08.16 remained the course record till 1997. Spedding's second place 2.08.33 secured the English record, which still stands. Allister Hutton, a winner in the making, finished third, improving his PB by almost seven minutes. In the women's race, Ingrid Kristiansen's winning time of 2.21.06 was a world best. Beaten into second place, but still capturing the UK record with 2.28.06, was Sarah Rowell.

The strong winds of the 1986 race blew away the hopes cherished by Toshihiko Seko and Grete Waitz of world best times. Only one man ever headed Seko, and that was the pacemaker. Seko left the pacemaker behind just after Tower Bridge. His halfway split was 63.30, but when he turned into the wind at the 18th mile, the strain showed and he eventually crossed Westminster Bridge in 2.10.02. Hugh Jones (inside 2.12 for the ninth time) and Allister Hutton followed him home. Waitz's 2.24.54 was a lifetime best. She finished six minutes ahead of New Zealand's Mary O'Connor.

Japan was to take the crown again in 1987, this time in the shape of Hiromi Taniguchi (2.09.50). Nechadi El Mostafa (Morocco) got the best of a real scrap to hold off a sprinting Hugh Jones. In the women's race, Ingrid Kristiansen returned to take her third London title in 2.22.38 after an attempt on her own world best had left her too much to do in the second half of the race. Priscilla Welch took the UK record down to 2.26.51 in second place. Veronique Marot, a future winner for Britain, was third.

Another Olympic year came in 1988, with Kevin Forster

finishing second to Denmark's Henrik Jorgensen to secure a place for Seoul. There was a fourth triumph, this time in 2.25.41, for Ingrid Kristiansen in the women's race. Ann Ford, for Britain, was almost five minutes behind in second.

Five of the top eight in Seoul were on the start line for 1989, but it was world champion Douglas Wakiihuri who took the title in 2.09.03, sprinting away on Westminster Bridge (the only time he'd led the race) to beat Steve Moneghetti of Australia. In the women's race, it was the 35-year-old Veronique Marot's year. Her 2.25.56 marked the biggest win of her career.

The tenth London Marathon, that of 1990, saw the first British men's winner since 1985 when Allister Hutton, now 35, left a quality field far behind after dropping the pacemaker at 14 miles and forging on in the poor weather to finish in 2.10.10. It was Hutton's first marathon win. The first five in the women's race all crossed the line in under 2.30, with Poland's Wanda Panfil getting there first in 2.26.31.

In 1991, London played host to the IAAF/ADT World Marathon Cup, the first time that an IAAF championship had been incorporated with an existing mass-participation race. The field was correspondingly strong. The relatively unknown Soviet runner Yakov Tolstikov broke away from a massive leading pack at 14 miles to win in 2.09.17. The team title went to the hosts, Great Britain. The great Portuguese runner Rosa Mota, reigning world and Olympic champion, won the women's race in 2.26.14. The women's team title went to the Soviet Union.

The next year it was the turn of former racing cyclist Antonio Pinto of Portugal, who clinched his first major title in his first London Marathon, in a time of 2.10.02. Katrin Dorre of Germany came home first in a slowish women's race in a time of 2.29.39.

The 1993 race highlighted the pre-race rivalry between Liz

McColgan of Scotland and Australia's Lisa Ondieki, but they were upstaged by the reigning champion. Katrin Dorre turned in a well-timed win in 2.27.09 after Ondieki found herself unable to match the German's finishing kick. McColgan had to settle for a slightly distant third. It was the first defeat of her marathon career, but she would be back.

As for the men's race, that went to an Englishman for the first time since 1984. Eamonn Martin, a car worker from Basildon, was making his debut at the distance after taking gold in the Commonwealth Games at 10,000 metres. He outsprinted the Mexican Isidro Rico on Westminster Bridge to cross the line in 2.10.50. It had been a good week for him. Days earlier, he had become father to Eamonn Junior.

In a race characterised by high winds, Mexico's Dionicio Ceron produced one of the finest London runs of all time to take the 1994 title in 2.08.53. Despite the conditions, Ceron stunned the world with a 14.41 split between 35 and 40 kilometres. The first five runners broke 2.10. Eighth, in 2.11.05, defending champion Eamonn Martin was top Briton. The women's race, marred by the conditions, featured a repeat of the previous year's one-two, with Katrin Dorre finishing ahead of Lisa Ondieki. It was Dorre's third successive title, though her 2.32.34 was the slowest winning time in the race's history.

Dionicio Ceron went on to retain his title in 1995 in an enthralling contest in which he and Steve Moneghetti reeled in Antonio Pinto after being over a minute down with 5 miles to go. The Mexican and the Australian went shoulder-to-shoulder until The Mall, where Ceron burnt off Moneghetti to record a 2.08.30 which was only fourteen seconds off Steve Jones's course record. It was the second time Moneghetti had found himself beaten by three seconds in London.

Katrin Dorre's reign as women's champion was finally ended by the relatively unsung Polish runner Malgorzata Sobanska, who grabbed a decisive ten-second lead in the closing stages to beat Manuela Machado of Portugal. Liz McColgan, struggling back to fitness after nearly three years dogged by injury, beat Dorre into sixth place.

A year later, McColgan truly was back. This, the 1996 race, was the hottest London Marathon ever and for much of the race McColgan stayed with the elite pack behind an early breakaway alliance let by Norway's Anita Hakenstad. McColgan only gained sight of her at 30k when, encouraged, she closed the gap inexorably. By the finish, McColgan was over two minutes clear of the rest of the field. The emerging Kenyan runner, Joyce Chepchumba, followed her home. McColgan had beaten her by a distance, but Chepchumba would return to avenge defeat. In the men's race, Dionicio Ceron crossed the finish line for his third win in as many years.

The 1997 marathon was memorable for the cruelty of the margin by which Joyce Chepchumba reversed the result of 1996. By dint of a characteristically gritty performance, McColgan had battled her way up to Chepchumba and started a long drive for home as she turned off the Embankment. By the time she entered The Mall, the Scot looked to have the race in the bag but Chepchumba miraculously gathered herself for a final push. She overtook McColgan virtually on the line. She was the winner by one second. The effort of that last sprint left her vomiting. McColgan gave her runner's-up medal to a child in the crowd. She'd already got several of those at home, she said.

The men's race was another nail-biter. Steve Jones's twelve-year-old course record was finally eclipsed in a finish in which the winner was in doubt until the last strides. Antonio Pinto came from way back in the closing miles to grab victory from Stephano Baldini – 2.07.55 beat 2.07.57. Eight of the first ten set personal bests, including Richard Nerurkar in 2.08.36 in fifth place.

Ireland's Catherina McKiernan was odds-on favourite to

take the 1998 women's race after recording the fastest-ever debut marathon in Berlin in September 1997. Approaching 17 miles, the 29-year-old Dublin-based runner broke away from defending champion Joyce Chepchumba and 1996 winner Liz McColgan to overhaul the race leaders Lidia Simon and Adriana Fernandez. She surged on unchallenged to win in 2.26.26. McColgan and Chepchumba followed her home.

Six miles from the finish, the unfancied outside Abdelkader El Mouaziz looked set for a surprise victory in the men's race when he broke away to set up a 40-yard lead. But world champion Abel Anton overhauled him in the last mile, running 2.07.57 to miss Antonio Pinto's 1997 record, and a $25,000 bonus, by two seconds. He might have made it had he not waved at the crowd on his way down The Mall. El Mouaziz was second and Pinto third.

The Course

There are three starts for the London Marathon, and which one you line up at will depend on such factors as ability, age, ambition and apparel. For instance, if you are intending to run London dressed as a tree, a centipede, the Queen or a man sitting on a toilet, you will almost certainly go from pen 7 or 8 of Red Start, home of all that is novel and fancy in running outfits.

The line for the Red Start of 1999 was drawn, as ever, on Charlton Way, just outside the gates of Greenwich Park. Charlton Way is the jumping-off point for the mass field as well as overseas runners. With a queue to exit the constricted gateway that stretches down the park almost to General Wolfe's statue, it is the slowest place to depart from but visually the most fun. Wombles, rhinos and a human tub of pot noodles are no bad distraction when you are skewered on the rack of first-timer's nerves.

Blue Start goes from Shooter's Hill Road, which bisects Blackheath and which on every other day of the year is a traffic-choked main route out of south-east London. From here go the elite women and men, the wheelchair athletes, and the field for the UK Athletics and Amateur Athletics Association of England Championships. Some of the mass field go from there too. Green Start sets off from St John's Park, Blackheath, and is the launchpad for 'Fast for Their Age' veterans, men over 60, women over 55, and the Football Challenge runners.

I've begun every one of my marathons from Red Start, making a blindside dash by the barriers to squeeze into pen 6 so I can cross the start before the clock ticks into double figures. The first half-mile is crowded and, of necessity, leisurely. If you're a first-timer, the sheer dawdling enormous endlessness of the stream of runners will fill you with awe, excitement and impatience.

The Green line joins Blue at the junction of Shooter's Hill with Old Dover Road. They get Charlton Park Lane, the appealingly named Ha-Ha Road and Grant Depot to themselves, while Red starters file along one of the prettiest parts of the course, through spring-leafy Charlton Village where residents have set up picnic tables and chairs on front lawns to enjoy the grandstand view (and deter runners from using their gardens as temporary urinals). The third mile is surprisingly switchback-like, with a sudden, steep hill that asks searching questions about your training. Remember to grab a drink at the water station; especially if you're at the back of the pack, you'll have some long, hot hours ahead.

It's around here that the course passes the Woolwich Artillery Barracks, which has the longest Georgian façade in Europe but which for runners is, more importantly, John Wilson Street, a great downhill canter to the roundabout and the first of the jazz bands. Red joins Green and Blue. The course is wide here, and most people feel fresh and optimistic; it's easy to be seduced into a faster pace that you'll regret later.

You go along Woolwich Church Street and Woolwich Road, with The Valley, Charlton's stadium, tucked in the dip to the left. The road narrows and darkens. You're about to duck under the ugly, massive flyover on which traffic thunders towards the Blackwall Tunnel. You emerge into a road of modest terrace houses, shops, the concrete monstrosity that is Greenwich Hospital and then the Arches Leisure Centre. Time to refuel again at the water station outside its front steps. Six miles accomplished.

This is an elegant part of the route. On the right stands the Royal Naval College, on the left the huge lawns and ancient pillared façade of Inigo Jones's Queen's House. You swing to the right sharply and find yourself suddenly jostling in the bottleneck round the *Cutty Sark*. This is one of the most crowded parts of the course, a prime spot for spectating.

Next comes the long uphill hike of Creek Road, followed by Evelyn Street and a tour of the smart, suburban developments round Surrey Quays. It's a quiet part of the race here. Runners have settled into the task; the big crowds are waiting for them further along the route. You'll start to encounter them around the 11-mile mark when you pass near the mouth of the Rotherhithe Tunnel. Jamaica Road is a bright, flat stretch with plenty of standing room for friends and family to cheer you on. You've got Tower Bridge coming up. Most people feel good here; you're coming up to the halfway mark, you'll have done 13 miles; another 13 to go, but right now that doesn't seem so hard.

And now a few words about London 98. When people who ran that one get together, they sooner or later ask the big question: Where were you when the hailstorm started? I was in Cable Street. And I was in it for possibly the last time ever, because for London 99 the organisers changed the route.

Cable Street had always been a kind of runners' Hickstead Derby: a mile-long obstacle course of traffic islands, lamps, bins, bumps and lumps along which the pack, which had thinned out comfortably over Tower Bridge, was suddenly filtered through an eleven-foot-wide corridor and concertinaed by the resulting mass deceleration into a uniquely hazardous experience involving the kiss of toecaps against your heel and unsolicited palms between your shoulder blades. When the hailstorm came in 1998 it was like being stuck in a crowded lift, the ceiling of which had been peeled off so someone could pelt you with hunks of frozen snow.

That said, I'd always had a particular affection for this part of the course. Some good people from my club, the East End Road Runners, would station themselves on a street corner under their Ribena-coloured banner and shout encouraging words to anyone who passed by wearing a purple vest. When you've run nearly 14 miles and you've got nearly as many left in front of you to go, there's nothing like a line of familiar faces to swear at. (And even if you didn't belong to the club, just running in purple would guarantee you a hell of a reception at least once along the route.)

But London 99 was going to be different. Instead of running through what seemed like a permanent exhibition of street furniture, we were due to pass eastbound along The Highway. This would be partitioned so that after hanging a left at Butcher Row and rejoining the traditional route, the one which takes in Commercial Road, West India Dock Road and Poplar High Street before venturing into the tough near-endlessness of the Isle of Dogs, we would eventually pass up Narrow Street and rejoin The Highway westbound around the 21-mile mark.

It made sense. The great Cable Street bottleneck had always been a safety hazard and a squanderer of precious minutes. This way, too, spectators in The Highway would get the chance to see two races simultaneously, with runners going both ways for a good hour-and-a-half. You wondered, though, how the new set-up would impact on the slower runners. Would the view of fleeter folk passing in the other direction be an inspiration or something more like a final straw?

The 6-mile stretch round the Isle of Dogs is where things start getting hard, particularly if you haven't notched up enough of the long runs in training. Here, pounding tinnily over the metal approach bridge to Canary Wharf, is where even if you are a fully accredited misanthropist you feel grateful for the support of other runners. By now you are all struggling to cope with a combination of physical and psychological deterioration. There are tantalising glimpses of normal life going on; a few yards away from you, newspapers are publishing and people in suits, with groomed hair and no sweat slicks down their fronts, are crossing the road to go and sit in wine bars. Another world.

You head for Marsh Wall, and go past the little toytown train stations of Crossharbour and Mudchute to the very tip of the Isle of Dogs. From here, the route runs alongside the Thames, all the way back up this U-shaped Calvary via Westferry Road. At the top you plunge into the cool, echoing, oil-pungent darkness of an underground round-about. Your mind registers dampness, litter, marshals gesticulating to ensure you leave at the correct exit. When you come out, you are struck by the brightness. It is not just the suddenness of the daylight. You also know that you have done the best part of 20 miles. You have made it to Limehouse.

Narrow Street is another fetching part of the route. If you are going to fall apart – and this is where many runners have to grapple with the wall – it might as well be here, forcing yourself into a survival shuffle past the Grapes pub and the grassy new park that hides the Limehouse Link road tunnel. Twenty-one miles done. Now comes your second crack at

The Highway, this time in the opposite direction. Be thankful that the crowd which gathers here are amongst the friendliest and most warmly appreciative of all London. They will have been waiting for you since early in the morning. Try not to grimace at them.

By now, the yellow and red mile markers can be playing jokes on you; every time you look up at them, they move backwards. If you are suffering, it will be hard to take in your surroundings. Between Thomas More Street and St Katharine's Dock you'll probably just register a blur of posh, pale buildings, a series of cricked roads that lead inexorably to the Tower of London and with it one of the marathon's most famed experiences.

There are 400 metres of cobblestones, covered though not entirely muffled by carpet. You'll encounter a bunch of official race photographers here. Paranoid, you will imagine that they have chosen this spot to capture your discomfort as you jolt and stumble over the old stones. You will decide to foil them by bestowing your widest smile. This is why everyone who runs over the cobblestones seems to be in the grip of an almost deranged hilarity.

Lower and Upper Thames Street, with those high office buildings and overhead bridges, can seem dark and interminable to the tired runner, while the Blackfriars underpass which follows brings moments of crazy elation. Only a couple or so more miles, and then you can party. But be warned, they can seem the longest miles you have ever run. It's here, along the Victoria Embankment, that you can put into practice all those psychological tricks you have learnt in training: telling yourself that you're just setting out on a little early-morning run, that your clothes are dry and fresh, that your toenails aren't about to drop off.

At Westminster Bridge you turn right. Just Great George Street and Birdcage Walk remain to be survived now. The commentary from the P.A. system floats towards you, over the trees of St James's Park. It's almost over. Only another 0.2 left to go. Turning the corner into The Mall you are aware of a large grey building on your left, behind high railings, but raising a final sprint seems more important than drinking in this view of Buckingham Palace. For most runners, what draws their gaze instead is one of the most welcome sights they have ever had the chance to witness: the finish line of the London Marathon.

Running by Numbers

Top ten occupations for people running the 1999 London Marathon

1 Students (1,991)
2 Teachers (1,760)
3 Accountants (1,200)
4 Military services (1,158)
5 Film-makers (1,056)
6 Police (958)
7 Consultants (922)
8 Building trade (873)
9 Sales managers (847)
10 Administrators (768)

Bottom ten occupations for people running the 1999 London Marathon

1 Dental assistants (19)
2 Politicians (22)
3 Stock Exchange (28)
4 Waiters (33)
5 Electricians (35)
6 Psychiatrists (35)
7 Haulage workers (40)
8 Financial analysts (42)

9 Librarians (54)
10 Economists (58)

Top ten nationalities of people given places in 1999

1 Great Britain and Northern Ireland (39,509)
2 France (700)
3 USA (659)
4 Germany (364)
5 Italy (240)
6 Netherlands (217)
7 Switzerland (130)
8 Belgium (107)
9 South Africa (99)
10 Sweden (98)

Ten popular costumes worn by charity runners

1 Big Ben
2 8ft pirate
3 Rhino
4 8-man centipede
5 Man sitting on toilet
6 Tree
7 The Queen
8 Womble
9 Camel
10 Pot Noodles

Odd numbers

1 £millions raised by charity runners (1981–98)
15.7
2 Number of people who ran for charity in
1998 23,000
3 Fastest MP ever to have run London: Matthew
Parris (1985) 2.32.57

4 Total amount in litres of sweat lost by particip-
ants in a marathon   120,000

5 Number of people called Dave running in 1999
marathon   1,705

 6 Number of running Smiths   453

 7 Number of running Joneses   363

 8 Number of runners dressed as Elvis   3

 9 Oldest runner (male) Abraham Weintraub (89)

10 Oldest runner (female) Jenny Wood Allen (87)

Behind the scenes

 1 Finisher's medals   30,000

 2 Goody bags for runners   30,000

 3 Lorries transporting runners' kit   50

 4 Barriers   8,500

 5 Barriers in metres 16,000

 6 Marshalls at start   1,100

 7 Marshalls on course   3,050

 8 Marshalls at finish   2,500

 9 Water station volunteers   2,000

10 Litres of blue paint   100

Creature comforts

 1 Portable toilets   500

 2 Lbs of petroleum jelly   88

 3 Bottles of Vittel water   625,000

 4 Pouches of Liquid Power   130,000

 5 Water stations   23

 6 Special drink stations for elite runners   8

 7 Showers   4

In case of emergency

 1 St John Ambulance Volunteers   1,500

 2 Ambulances   68

3 First Aid Stations   41
4 Stretchers   500
5 Physiotherapists   50
6 Podiatrists   30
7 Foil blankets   5,000
8 Cotton wool balls   5,000
9 Vomit bags   1,000

Ten problems suffered by runners

1 Blisters
2 Cramp
3 Skin abrasions
4 Black toenails
5 Dehydration
6 Sprains
7 Chafing
8 Runner's trots
9 Pulled muscles
10 Broken ankles

Ten famous sights on the course

1 The Ranger's House, Greenwich
2 The Royal Naval Hospital
3 The *Cutty Sark*
4 The Mayflower pub
5 Tower Bridge
6 Canary Wharf
7 The Tower of London
8 Cleopatra's Needle
9 Big Ben
10 Buckingham Palace

Hottest London Marathons pre-1999 (midday figures)

1   1996   21C (69.80F)

2 1986 17C (62.60F)
3 1988 16.4C (61.52F)
4 1985 14.1C (57.38F)
5 1982 14C (57.20F)

Five ways of coping with heat and humidity (advice for the average runner)

1 Run to finish, not to compete; don't be macho
2 Drink at every water station
3 Wear sunblock
4 Cool yourself at one of the shower stations. You can also pour your water instead of drinking it, but be considerate of other runners' safety
5 Be a woman. Female performance does not deteriorate as much as men's on a hot day, possibly because they do not sweat quite as much

Ten things runners do immediately after finishing the London Marathon

1 Collect winner's medal and cheque for $55,000
2 Stop still just beyond finish and be unable to move another step
3 Burst into tears
4 Move very slowly and stiffly through park to join up with friends and family
5 Go into nearest pub and drink enormous amounts of beer
6 Discover their eyebrows are encrusted with salt
7 Vow never to run anywhere ever again
8 Vow to train properly for next year's London
9 Mentally adjust their finish time downwards to allow for two toilet stops and the time they stopped to embrace member of family in Jamaica Road
10 Feel fantastically proud of themselves

Making Metal Work for You

A lot of things that have happened to me come down to decisions made earlier for what at the time seem to be completely unrelated reasons. Why London 99 turned out for me the way it did, for instance, can probably be traced back to the third weekend in March.

I was studying part-time for a diploma in counselling and the final day of the course coincided with the Brentwood Half-Marathon. I had been a student on the course for almost a year now and had grown close to the other students. It represented a part of my life which I would never be able to repeat.

In addition, I'd always had a problem with the way I ended things, walking away when they got difficult or boring, or when I'd loved something so much that by not saying goodbye I could pretend that it was not really over. I wanted to end this thing properly.

On the other hand, I liked the Brentwood Half-Marathon. It was timed perfectly to provide an accurate gauge of what I'd be capable of in London. The first two miles of the race were downhill and the previous year I'd done a PB. At a couple of points during the race, I'd met people I'd met during races before, which enhanced my sense of self as a member of the running community. And I'd finished ahead of my training partner, with whom I enjoyed a friendly, though unspoken, rivalry.

So I was emotionally tugged and, right up to a couple of days before Brentwood, I still didn't know whether I was going to run it or not, and the uncertainty was beginning to get to me. In the end I woke up on the Sunday and felt more like a counsellor than a runner. I went off to attend the last day of my course, and arranged to go for a run with Jessamy Calkin that night when I got back home. We would not be running very far or fast, or for very long. I would just have to make up the miles, with maybe an extra speedwork session, later.

Over the preceding two months, I'd got to know Jessamy. She was the friend of a friend who came up with her name when asked to suggest the most unlikely, reluctant and unrewarding candidate possible on whom to bestow the London Marathon entry which I had at my disposal.

My fantasy had, of course, been that Jessamy would experience an epiphany somewhere on the road to Red Start and discover for herself running's world of wonders; the way it cleared your head and widened your focus, the way it energised you and tranquillised you at the same time, how youthfully lean it made your body, how every run seemed to bring with it new insights and how sometimes it was like falling in love for the first time, the way it made you look at what was around you with new eyes.

But Jessamy doggedly refused to be converted. Her hatred of running only increased by proximity. Unable to get out of her commitment on medical grounds (broken back, dodgy ankle, past history as a speed freak) there seemed to be no escape for her.

That night in March, Jessamy and I set out for our run. It was around half-past seven, not long after dark. She spent the first mile abusing me roundly. I was held entirely responsible for everything from the hilly nature of south-east London to the unstylish nature of running apparel. I upped the pace to 8-minute miling so she couldn't run and talk at the same time, but she simply stuck with her grim-faced shuffle and griped at my disappearing back. Two miles into the run, at the foot of Lee Road where there is a line of interesting little shops and alleyways, Jessamy shot without looking across a concealed exit at the exact moment a car emerged.

Even if the driver hadn't managed to stop in time, the car hadn't been going very fast. An injury of just enough seriousness – reasonably dramatic contusions, say, or a hairline fracture – would have got Jessamy out of jail while still enabling her to carry out her duties as a mother, editor and luncher. Furthermore, as she was so keen on cars, I liked the idea of its being a car which rescued her from this commitment held in such loathing and dread, and at the time I wondered if she had some mysterious ability to make metal work for her. But it wasn't to be. The car had stopped. We were left to trundle on. She was doomed to run the London Marathon.

Almost built for the sport – wheelchair athlete Tushar Patel

Ready for more – Caroline
Taraskevics with her medal

Target achieved –
Flo Gibson at the finish

Eyes wide shut – Helen Spriggs
on the loneliest journey

Mutual support –
Gail Nerurkar with
husband Richard

True to herself and confident – Jayne Pope on the track

Man with a mission
– John Eusden

A good life now – Joe Fell

Still with the wheels on
– Chris Vernon

And now to slip quietly into middle age – Sophie Mirman (*right*) with her friend Polly

Looking to the future – Karen Hutchings

Dedicated in their training – Ian Hudspith (*left*) and big brother Mark

Awesome in their achievements – Anthony Read (*left*) and Tony Evans

On the road –
Kevin Wood (*left*)
and Steve Wehrle

Ton up –
Max Jones finishes
his 100th Marathon

Better by car – Jessamy Calkin with her idea of freedom

Being There – 18 April 1999

I live 600 metres from Red Start these days and as usual was in demand as a landlady by out-of-town friends looking for an extra hour's sleep and the chance to attend to pre-race bodily needs without a queue of two dozen nervous-bladdered strangers hopping up and down outside the door. I got breakfast for everybody. It was a displacement activity. I always find the mood before London to be portentous and ambivalent, like waiting for a wedding and funeral simultaneously. The task ahead seems so vast and unimaginable that it's tempting to escape by not thinking about it at all. Consequently an hour or so later, where the road dips then rises on the way out of Charlton Village, I find myself taken completely by surprise: 'Bloody hell, I'm running the London Marathon again.' This is followed by a feeling of dismay: 'And there's another 23 miles to go.'

I suppose this is the drawback of living so close to the marathon; there is so little scope for the chain of ritual events which helps time pass before you arrive at the start line, no journey from Charing Cross, no assembly with your club-mates at a traditional meeting place. Once you've pinned on your number and enrobed in your black bin-liner that's it, really.

We walked towards Greenwich Park. The grass on the heath was cool and damp and the sun was out, though obliterated by an inflatable of remarkable size and hideousness. It was advertising a supermarket. I hated that. And then, well, one minute you're a group and the next you aren't. You go into the private place called your head. I did my usual blindside sidle from pen 7 to 6. The hooter went. I stood, shuffled forward, stopped and shuffled again. The air was chilly and the oaks of the park took our light. People struggled out of bin-liners and old tops at the last minute and threw them against barriers. Our line broke into a jog. I squeezed through the left-hand gateway, the narrow one I use every April. Here it was bright and warm, all sky. On the kerbstones of Charlton Way the dates of past starts are marked in paint. I counted them down: 96, 97, 98, years of my life. Eleven minutes were already on the clock as I began to run the last London Marathon of the twentieth century.

Chris Vernon

It was Chris's sixteenth London. Through January he'd competed in the V50 category in a full cross-country and road-racing programme with his club, and by the end of the month he was writing 'Sore throat and cold' most days in his training log. He'd also run $9\frac{1}{2}$ miles cross-country in 76.38 in the South of England Championships at Parliament Hill Fields. It rained non-stop and oh, the mud. He should have worn spikes.

He did a 15-miler with the club the next day, stiff afterwards. First week in February, he logged a 49-mile week including the Vets AC Cross-Country on Wimbledon Common. Five miles, that was. Actually, probably only 4.8. Ran it a minute slower than last year, but he did cycle there and back from Dulwich. The next day was crisp and bright and he ran with his friend Richard from Dulwich to Hyde Park and back via Battersea Park – 24 miles, 3.31.

He was shattered by the Wednesday of the week after. He

gave himself a break, apart from cycling and a yoga session. On the 14th it was the Essex 20. 'Cold day. Flat course. Some wind. Beat Richard,' he noted in his training log. He felt better as the race went on, though, which was a good sign. It was the club championship. He was 2nd V50, behind Joe Fell.

Towards the end of February, he did his first four-hour training run. Four hours one minute, to be precise. Twenty-six miles. And a week after that, in the last round of the club championship, in the Surrey Cross-Country League on Wimbledon Common, he finished 0/50 *Champion*. And beat his friend Bernard by miles.

In March, he went up to Wales with the club. They did a 32-mile sponsored bike ride round Snowdon. They thought their legs would drop off but they recovered after much beer. The next day they ran in the forest in the pouring rain with hangovers. They meant to do two hours, but enthusiasm dropped off a bit after 8 miles.

He did the Fleet Half-Marathon in 1.33.16 on the 21st. Steady run, 7-minute miles all the way, felt OK. He was second 0/50 to Joe Fell again, and had a sore knee afterwards. Now he was going to start tapering for the Two Oceans in South Africa.

That Wednesday night, he did the club run steady. The knee seemed OK. He was breaking in his new Asics racers. Near the end of that week, he did a fast 3 miles, then a slow 8 the next day with his wife Sue before the flight to Cape Town. A day later, he was running alongside the ocean, drinking in a beautiful sunset.

The Two Oceans was on Easter Saturday, and it was exciting: being abroad with a bunch of clubmates, taking on a very tough race, the conditions hot and hilly. A 35-miler; he did 5.04. And they had a super holiday. And he was three minutes quicker than the year before.

He hadn't set out to do a faster time. He was running with

a friend from the club, and he'd trained this friend, who needed convincing that he could get round. Then, with a mile and a half to go, he came across another friend from the club: Bob Bell. He caught Bob when Bob was having a little walk. It was stinking hot. Bob had stopped at a water station and Chris passed him. After the race he was accused of barging Bob, but the subsequent steward's enquiry exonerated him because Bob shouldn't have been walking in a running race anyway. And Bob was thirteen years younger.

He came back to England and didn't do much in the two weeks left before London, just a little bit of jogging and, on the Sunday before, 5 miles which felt fast but weren't really. It's a thing he did before a marathon. He had to turn his legs over with some speed. But it was difficult to motivate himself, having just done South Africa. And bearing in mind it was his sixteenth London it wasn't as new and exciting as it had once been. And he was somewhat apprehensive because he always wondered if the wheels would come off, and when.

Chris Vernon's marathon

Registration is when you start to get hyped up. Touring the foreign marathon stands to see what the next one's going to be. I watched the Chicago video and picked up entry forms for the Dublin and the Comrades. You meet lots of friends and they're all asking you what you're going to do. And there's always one club member who hasn't made up his mind. Having gone through all the business of paying his entry money, getting a number, coming up to registration, he's saying, 'Well, I'll make up my mind on Saturday.'

I enjoy the hype of big events. Some people go into their shells and start telling you how awful they feel, and they've just had flu, and they've got this injury to their knee. When anyone asks me, I'm always going to do that one great run.

I went back to Dulwich and met people at the club to make final arrangements – which pub to meet in afterwards, and how people were going to get to the start, and how to meet at the start, and that sort of thing. So the build-up was well under way. That's why I like the big city marathons – all the rituals make a sense of occasion. Running a marathon is an occasion. It's not just any old 10k.

My cousin came to stay the night before. He was running his second marathon. He's in his early 50s. Turned up very late, having got lost, and then he needed totally organising – his kitbag, his number, what to wear, everything.

I'd long since prepared. It's my ritual the night before. Pin my number on with my special little gold pins that I've used for every marathon. One in each corner. Cut the holes in your black plastic bin-liner. Get out the socks you're going to wear. The shoes you're going to wear. The Vaseline – always essential for nipples and crutch. The track-suit trousers. The clean, dry underpants. Nothing is worse than going around in your wet, sodden shorts after a marathon. So in the morning nothing is left to chance. Which was just as well with my cousin staying. I was dishing out tips well into the night.

I slept quite well. You have to have settled all the arrangements, though. Where people are going to meet you. Have you got money for the tube? Beer money? Are you going to be hot/wet/cold after the race? A change of clothes for every eventuality, and what you don't use you put on the baggage bus. Then in the morning you can concentrate on enjoying it and meeting people and soaking up the atmosphere.

Sunday morning. The usual ritual. Get up at six. Breakfast of cereal and honey sandwiches, like Joyce Smith. And a cup of coffee. All to have been consumed three hours before the start, so I have to have finished by six-thirty. Then get dressed.

Sue gave me a lift to Blackheath. Dropped me off in the village. You walk over the heath in full sight of the balloons and the people. And then meet everybody else by the bandstand in Greenwich Park. Dump your stuff on the baggage bus. A little bit of a warm-up. But the secret of my start will never be revealed. Suffice to say it never takes me long to cross the line.

Having said that, I had a slow start this year – took me over a minute. I didn't want to be right up at the front, but I was a bit miffed to see they'd put all the foreign numbers at the front including five South African women who were race-walking.

It was cold, dry, no wind. I felt fine, just slow after the Two Oceans. I could *not* run quicker than 8-minute miles. I hardly did one mile under 8 minutes. Normally I would have expected to bowl along at 7.30 as long as possible, but once I got to the 6-mile mark I was doing fractionally over 8 all the way, and then slowed to 8.30s towards the end. But I felt so comfortable. It was a stroll in the park.

I met people along the way. In Jamaica Road there's always Stefan of Dulwich Runners, with his club umbrella so we can spot him. Lots of unrecognisable shouts from the crowd until the Dulwich Runners' support point at $13\frac{1}{2}$ miles. Great shouts from all the club members who weren't running. Coming up to Canary Wharf there's always Reiko, a Dulwich Runner who waves her flag with the Rising Sun. So I stopped and gave her a kiss. Yes, I was pretty foul by then.

Those fleeting conversations you have with the person next to you in a marathon. You come and go in their life, and they in yours: 'I'm bored, I want someone to talk to.' Afterwards, they'll be saying, 'Thank God he's gone! I met this awful man who couldn't stop talking.'

I ran alongside Sally Dawson of Herne Hill Harriers at 17 miles and we had a chat. She reminded me that we'd met at exactly the same point two years back, when she fell apart. Around 18 miles I saw this guy with '100 Marathon Club' on his back. He probably wasn't much older than I am but he looked so uncomfortably stiff that I vowed then and there that I was never going to run 100 marathons, that I was going to give up before my body got like that. I drifted up and he proudly told me it was his 125th. He looked as though it was his 1,000th.

Then I spotted Keith from the Stragglers Club in Newbury, sitting on the same wall that he's sat on in Docklands for at least ten years. During which time the wall has been demolished and rebuilt, and he's still on top of it. The two-way Highway was an interesting innovation. I'd seen the leaders, the top men's runners, 7 miles in front of me. And when I got to the 21-mile point there was a rhino coming through the halfway.

At 22 miles I caught the pink fairy. I do expect to be finishing my marathons ahead of pink fairies and Big Bens but it's getting closer and closer every year. Then the Tower of London. If I've been emotional, it's when the crowds are close and you can feel them pressing in on you, but at the Tower of London it was just peace and quiet, away from the spectators.

I kept off the carpet so I could see where I was putting my feet. Coming out of the Tower I noticed a couple of army runners – officers – being served glasses of port on a silver tray by a Guardsman. It was a snapshot. Like a dream. The port being poured out of a decanter, the Guardsman addressing them as Sir. And then they ran on.

I came out at Lower Thames Street and onto that long, long straight bit into the underpass. I was feeling quite jolly. Running along the tunnel shouting a lot at people who'd started to walk. 'Come along! No good walking! Just because you think people can't see you!' They looked at me as if I was a piece of shit come in on their trainers.

Along the Embankment. Temperature quite nice. And then I caught Bob Bell again. With a mile and a half to go. *Déjà vu.* I couldn't believe it. I'd thought he would have been running with his wife, and miles behind. Seeing Bob inspired me to run quite quickly. I crept past him on the other side. Didn't want to be accused of barging him again. Gave him a ten-yard gap.

Then, going down Birdcage Walk, Roger Easterbrook, a really young guy, comes past me as though he's doing 800 metres. I thought, 'Has nobody told him that no one overtakes Chris Vernon in the last mile of a marathon?' He disappeared, off into the distance. He was zigzagging, in and out of the runners. I came round the corner. Very surprised to beat my last year's time by two seconds. 3.39.49. Absolute fluke.

Then the usual finishing rituals. Helped a poor girl who was incredibly badly cramped to get to the medical tent. On with the dry clothes and off to the pub to hear everybody else's stories.

I felt relieved, relieved that the wheels hadn't come off. It's always relief. There's always the fear of the pain. Supposing something really bad did happen. People battling physical limits, that's what the marathon is.

And I was relieved to have got round in one piece in a respectable time: five minutes quicker than my first marathon. It's reassuring when you get to my age. Time is beginning to slip by. I'm in the Cellulite Zone. I feel I've reached the stage when I'm running with women with lots of cellulite. Gone are the days when my name appeared on the results page of *The Times* on a Monday. All the brave talk about, 'I'm going to give up running when I can't run a 10k in 40 minutes,' has gone, and I'm still there. Anyway, I made *The Times* on the Tuesday. That's still pretty good.

Chris Vernon's marathon tip
Taper right down before the race to allow your body to recover from training and leave you fresh and raring to go for the race. The best thing that can happen is to pick up a minor

injury with two weeks to go which forces you not to run – not quite, but you know what I mean.

John Eusden

The marathon was going to be John's mission. It was going to spring him from the depression that had dogged him in the six years since the death of his father. He'd get his weight down and lose the Prozac. Most of all, he was going to finish something, for a change. That had always been his problem, finishing things. His mates teased him about it. Every time he started something, they'd say, 'When are you going to give up, John?' He couldn't not complete it, not this job. He'd told so many people he was going to do it. Even if he walked all the way and finished last, there was no way he was not going to cross that finish line.

The day he heard he'd got a place, he bought a pair of Nikes, top of the range because he was a big bloke and he thought that the more cushioning he had the more comfortable running would be. On the first of January he taped the *Runner's World* Get You Round schedule on the kitchen worktop. He ran for 20 minutes the first session, then 30 minutes the next, then built up to 3, 4 miles. He spent as much time on his feet as possible and put in hours at the gym. He was out of shape but he could do it. Once he'd been invited by the LTA to train in one of their junior squads. He'd been a good footballer and a promising skier. He was only 26 now. He'd get it back. But then he got shin splints.

It was his weight that was the trouble, of that he was sure. He did a 6-miler round Chigwell at the beginning of February and the first 5 were hell. Only when he came to the final mile on grass did he feel OK. It was like he was wearing slippers after all that concrete.

The next Sunday he went for a long run with some new

mates from the East End Road Runners. They were really fit, he couldn't believe it, they could talk and run at the same time. He did 5 miles with them and it started to hurt so he turned round and ran back. He was angry, he wanted to run and he couldn't. He wanted an injection to stop the pain, it was so bad.

On the Thursday of that week he went along to the East End Road Runners for their club night. It was the first time he'd ever been through the doors of a running club. He wasn't sure about it at first. He felt a bit inadequate. In they all came with their kitbags and their professional-looking stuff, while he'd just turned up in what he had on. But they were really helpful. It was unusual, that. Usually when you came in as a stranger, people were stand-offish and it took a bit of time before you found someone you could get on with. But they were all really friendly from the start.

He did some of the speedwork sessions, he'd got a whole lot quicker since the start of January, but the shin splints hurt again, so he had to pack up. He stood in the middle of the clubhouse and just said, 'Fuck, fuck, fuck,' because it felt like it was never going to be any different, he'd have barbed wire in his legs all the way to April, he'd never be able to train properly, he was going to have to give up. And then he was going to feel like a failure, the way he'd felt when he got the depression and couldn't go on with the City job. Haunted. Another opportunity missed.

'Fuck, fuck, fuck.'

'You'll be all right,' said a bloke called Andy. 'Motion control shoes is all you need.'

So he bought himself a pair of Sauconys. When he felt the back of them they were really hard, he couldn't believe he was going to be able to run in them, but they were so comfortable. He started building up the mileage again. In March he got work as a sparks on a building site up in Waterloo. At lunchtimes he went running along by the

Thames. A lot of the builders took the piss at first, and it was embarrassing running past young kids; it made him tense up. And all those other runners out there – he couldn't believe how fast they were going. They were sprinting. But he stuck to it. He told himself he didn't care how fast other people were. He was enjoying it, that was what mattered. He stopped getting the hump. That was unusual for him.

Still, the sparks job didn't leave him as much time for training as he'd have liked. Then he got a groin pull at the start of April, jumping on the back of a truck. It started to get to him again, his lack of confidence, his fear of failure. Wouldn't it just be best to forget about it? That's what people expected of him, after all. Good old John. Never finishes things. They could have a laugh about it.

He sat down and started reading *The Runner's Handbook*. He read about this guy who ran a marathon even though he was dying of cancer; the guy got one of his nephews who hadn't run before to run it with him. Did it in 4.40. Guts and determination. It inspired him, that did.

Sitting there with the book, he made out a race plan. Every mile marker he'd stop, have a drink, walk a bit. He needed to try and break it up. He'd station his wife Nicky and his kids and his mates at various points round the course. That way he'd have familiar faces to look forward to. And Nicky, she was going to meet him afterwards at the letter Z because she'd be easy to find there, there'd be no one at Z apart from a few Russians. All he had to do was get round. If he finished anywhere higher up the field than last, that'd be a bonus.

He closed the book. He felt suddenly there was something coming to him from the marathon. He felt the marathon was going to change him.

John Eusden's marathon
A mate of my sister-in-law's, he'd run a couple of marathons before and I was supposed to be meeting him at All Saints

Church on Blackheath but at five to nine he still wasn't there. So I thought, 'I'll go to the toilet and get ready.'

I hadn't realised how many people would be going to the toilet. Couldn't believe it. Thirty in each queue. A bloke was shouting, 'Get your baggage in the trucks,' and there was this queue, and I'm on my own, I'm trying to talk to a few people because I'm nervous, and then I see people putting Vaseline on their chests and nipples and I didn't have any. So there's a bloke with a bucket of the stuff and I said, 'Could I have some of that?' And then I made my way to the pens.

I looked at the corner of my number and I'm in number 1. I looked round and all I saw was Moroccans and Kenyans. Professionals. They were looking at me funny. The marshal looked me up and down – I was about three times the size of them – and he said, 'You're not in the right pen.' I said, 'Yeah, they made a mistake,' but part of me wanted to say, 'Yes, I am, you snotty bastard,' because of the way he was looking at me.

So I got into pen 4. Someone pulled the barrier open. They shut the gate. I looked up and saw a big yellow *Runner's World* stick saying, 'Target Time 3.30.' But it was two minutes before the start and I couldn't get out.

By the time I got to the first drink station, there was already none left. I'd got sucked in fast, running at their pace, it didn't do me any favours. Next to me a Scouse geezer was saying, 'I'm going to take it easy, do it in four and a half,' so I said, 'Yeah, that's what I'm doing.'

I was just amazed at the amount of spectators, sticking their hands out. When I got to 13 miles I wanted to kill them all. Halfway mark, people really annoying me. But just before Tower Bridge I had a drink and a little walk and then I came round the corner and up on the bridge and Nicky and Maisie were waiting for me. I got choked up then.

I had another little drink and a chat and set off again. When I was around the 14-mile mark, because of the way the course had been laid out I could see people coming back the other way, and they were already at 22 miles. There was only a barrier between us and them and I was thinking, 'Shit, shall I jump that barrier?' A geezer in front said the same thing to his mate. Normally that's the sort of thing I do, take short cuts. But I thought, 'No, I'm not going to do that this time. I'm going to do it straight.'

I got choked up quite a few times in the race. I needed to see people I knew because I was running on my own and my friends were waiting for me by the City Pride pub. I seen them twice. At 16 miles, my mate Ben looked really choked up. I thought, 'Oh, that's nice. He's seen me. He's upset for me.' But what happened was, he'd had a bad knee injury the week before, and just before I came along he'd jumped over a barrier with a plastic cup of lager in his mouth. Got lager all over himself and smashed his knee again, and he didn't want to speak to me because he was in agony himself.

Meanwhile, Ben was saying, 'D'you want your drink, d'you want your drink?' I shouted, 'Have a look at me, what d'you think?' Because I was in bits. So he was just looking at me with this hurt look on his face.

At 16 miles, a physio had a look at my feet. She said, 'Stop every mile if you want to finish.' By 20 miles I'd been walking quite a bit and I was feeling all right. I poured my bottle of water over my mate Chad's head. And when I got to the next drink station there was nothing left. I'd got a terrible headache. And that's when I started to think, 'I can't do this.' And then I see a blind man come past me and I thought, 'Fucking hell, if he can do it, I can.'

But around 21 miles I was really getting upset. I just wanted to lie down and go to sleep. I saw these people run past in orange T-shirts; they were collecting for a children's charity and the T-shirts were printed IN MEMORY OF MY SON . . . IN MEMORY OF MY DAUGHTER . . . Oh God.

Then I got to the cobblestones. When I'd left Nicky at Tower Bridge I'd said, 'See you by the cobblestones,' and I was thinking, 'Oh, I'll be all right there because of the carpet.' And by the time I got there the carpet was all rolled up. I was going along these cobblestones saying, 'This is fucking bollocks, this is fucking bollocks.' Talking to myself like a nutter.

The last three miles. That bit of the Embankment. Everyone knows that road so well. When I hit that 23-mile mark I knew there was 3.2 to go, and I'd drove down that road so many times I knew how far that 3.2 was, and that made it harder. I got to Parliament Square and there was a copper there and I said, 'How much further?' And he said, 'Ooh, about five miles.' I wasn't in the mood for jokes.

I saw the finish line. I put on a sprint. When they came to take my chip off, because I lose everything I'd laced it into my shoe, so I had to take my shoe off. And that was it. I couldn't move.

I managed to hobble to the baggage cart. I just wanted to cry, I just wanted to see Nicky and my family. But it was about half past four, I suppose. I took my shoes off and sat by the baggage cart and poured water over my feet. Then I went to St John and said, 'I can't move. I can't walk.'

He massaged my feet and said, 'Where are you going to meet your wife?'

'Z.'

'What are you, Russian or something?'

They put me in a wheelchair and wheeled me down to Z. Course, by the time I'd got in there was no one left in E anyway. In the wheelchair, I had my hands behind my head. Nicky thought I'd broken my neck. They put me in a cab on the swivel seat for disabled people, and we went to my sister-in-law's and had a bath and a pizza.

I started to feel good. Driving back from there it was like I'd been in a battle zone, I'd been to war, I'd been away for ages. I started to feel euphoric. When I'd first finished I was like, 'I'm not running again, I'm not running down the shops to buy a pint of milk, I'm not doing nothing,' but that night my sister rang from New York and said, 'Will you do the New York Marathon with me?' And I said, 'Yes.'

Straight after the race, I'd been in so much pain I couldn't feel good. It was only later that I started to realise what I'd done. I thought there'd probably only be a hundred people behind me at the end and it turned out there were thousands. I feel taller. I'm surprised how many people rang up to say congratulations. I was shocked. I didn't realise it was such an achievement. I do, I feel taller.

John Eusden's marathon tip
Don't just run your marathon, experience it.

Jayne Pope

Jayne was ambivalent about the London Marathon. It had been the scene of both dream runs and worst nightmares. Her first London ever, she'd been pleased to finish around 4.40. Since then she'd improved as a runner so dramatically she had qualified for elite status.

Last year's London had been hard, exhausting, disappointing, by her exacting standards. An awful spell at 21 miles when she had to walk. Never did she want to repeat that experience. On the other hand, she had now changed clubs and had a different training regime and a new training partner. By February, she was feeling optimistic and positive.

Racing went well. It usually did in February because there was a lot of cross-country, which she loved, and the Benfleet 15, which was semi-cross-country, and which she also loved. The weather was always bad, but this time it was particularly windy. She didn't mind. She just liked the course. She ran very well, considering she was taking it very easy because owing to her cross-country commitments it was the longest she'd run. First vet! And the Essex 20, she did very well there, too. Second vet! So, yes, she thought she might be on for a good London.

But March, that was so dispiriting. She was third vet at the Finchley 20 but she'd been tired since the start of the month. The old pattern reasserting itself. February was always an up. And by the end of March she was always completely knackered.

Very bad this year, it was. She did the Paddock Wood half-marathon and she just couldn't run properly. She went round very, very slowly. She found herself thinking, 'Mentally, I've had enough. That's what it is.'

But she couldn't understand it, why she should be tired. All she knew was, she was just drained. She ought to be on top of her fitness by now, and she couldn't accept that she wasn't.

Jayne Pope's marathon

I was feeling great in the days before the race but not looking forward to it at all, because I knew what that 21-mile point is like. It's the mental thing, really. In my third London I did 3.13, and after that it got worse. At 21 miles last year I walked, though I still did 3.25. This year I was looking at it as a chore.

I had a plan. I thought I'd do a very slow 10k and then a fast 20-miler. I went from elite start; I knew some people there. They went shooting off, so I ran with a girl who was from the army. I did $7\frac{1}{2}$-minute miling. I met the people who'd gone shooting off later on.

The first 10k was just a breeze. I enjoyed it immensely because it was so slow. I don't usually race at that speed. Then I started the 20-miler. I broke that up into 5-mile pieces and upped it to 7.20-minute miling. Comfortable, that was.

Then I caught up somebody I'd met who I'd beaten in the last three races, and started running with her. She hadn't trained this year, but she was a sub-three marathoner. Tower Bridge – lovely. Canary Wharf – that was getting a bit tough. But it was actually OK till I remembered how I felt last year and then it started coming back again exactly like last year, and come mile 21 it was just . . . my head. I was scared, I was drowned, my energy left me. I started walking; I couldn't run. My legs were dead. It's so frustrating! You just haven't got it!

I never walked continuously. I fartlek it. Run, walk, run walk. Takes too long otherwise. I just wanted to get it over with. The fast men were coming in with me. They were so kind. They put their hands behind my back to push me in: 'Come on, love, don't give up here.' I was completely exhausted. I got in at 3.26, in bits. As I crossed the finish line, I just thought, 'Oh shit, my legs.'

The people giving out the medals were so lovely. I said, 'Oh my God, I feel awful,' and they said, 'People come in here and say they've done a worse time than last year, and they've still done a good time.' I suppose that put things in proportion. But I thought, 'How come that happened to me today, being like a cripple and getting all that sympathy from the men, when other times I'd come charging through?' And five weeks later I ran Prague, and I started with 7.35-minute miling for the first 6 miles, then just picked it up. It was like racing a 20-miler. Effortless. No pressure. Because I hadn't been there before and I didn't know what was coming. I never stopped once and I finished in 3.20.

It's a funny distance, isn't it? You need so much strength mentally and physically, because it breaks you down. That 21-mile thing in London – it's like you're approaching a torture, and you don't want to go into the torture room again. And it's that fear which paralyses you.

Only in London. Because I wouldn't get that in any other

race, because on other races I've never been there before. But I've been there in London and it's like, 'Why am I doing this to myself again? Because I'm forfeiting all my good training and all my good times; I'm taking my confidence away from me.'

I don't know anybody else who reacts this way. Some people do it time and time again and they don't seem to be affected. Maybe I'm not mentally strong enough. Then again, I heard one of the international men say he had a really bad experience in the Boston Marathon, and once you've had one of those you don't want to repeat it.

I just felt drained. Unnaturally so. As if I'd been through some horrendous ordeal. I just find the crowd all too much. I don't need to be shouted at and clapped on. When I compare it to the other marathons I've run, the others were pleasure, plain sailing. I'm not doing London again.

A few days after London I talked to my coach and he looked at my times for 10ks and half-marathons and said, 'You're faster over shorter distances.' So I'd decided to go for a couple of half-marathons in the summer, but first, I thought, I'd do Prague. And I'm so glad I did because it was exciting. Exhilarating. It was a lift. I've got my taste for marathons back.

Jayne Pope's marathon tip
Run your own race and don't get tugged along by other people.

The Hudspith Brothers

Mark's racing and preparation went well. Already an established force in UK marathon running, he had created a surprise at the 1994 Commonwealth Games by taking the bronze medal after placing seventeenth in that year's London with 2.12.52. In London the following year he finished eleventh with 2.11.58. Since then, he'd struggled to recapture that form, but now he was confident about his chances of achieving not just the 2.14 finish which would qualify him for the World Championships, but a PB. For kid brother Ian, though, it was a different story.

Ian was going for his first marathon after several years of success at the shorter distances. He'd celebrated the New Year by winning the Morpeth–Newcastle 14.1, beating Mark by a toecap or so. But after that, the build-up was far from ideal.

He picked up an injury in mid-January. Knee. Tendinitis. He'd had a week easy after the Morpeth–Newcastle but probably came back too quickly. Anyway, he broke down. He missed three weeks.

It was frustrating. Especially when it was an injury like tendinitis, because you couldn't put a timescale on it. He ran with it for a week. Niggly, that's what it was. It came on during runs.

He had pretty intensive physiotherapy for a couple of weeks and he was doing little bits and pieces here and there, like some exercise bike at work. But it wasn't the same. Swimming was too much hassle. It was boring. He only liked running.

So no, the preparation didn't go fantastic. After he got back from that knee injury he didn't train as well as he had in the past. He was running OK, but not as well as he had done. His big brother was beating him in every race when normally he'd beat Mark in one and Mark would beat him in the next. So now the marathon had come round he wasn't exactly brimming with confidence.

Ian Hudspith's marathon

We went down to register on the Friday; we came on the train. We stayed at Tower Bridge Hotel and picked our numbers up there because we were elite. Mum and Dad came across for a meal the night before the race. Pizza in Leicester Square; we always go there. On the corner, next to the Sussex pub. I had lasagne, though it wouldn't matter, would it, if you had a pizza? You'd be taking it to the extreme if you refused a pizza. A lot of runners talk till the cows come home about their diet but they'd be better off if they just got out and did more running.

I didn't sleep that night. I couldn't make it to sleep till one and we were up at six. But you can get away with one not great night's sleep. I sat in the elite athletes' tent chatting with the lads. Did a light jog. A bit of sweating. I had a few blisters, so I'd taped them up.

I was looking for a time of 2.14 to 2.15. I ran in the third group. My pacemaker did his job spot on. Colin Moore. He was told to take the group through halfway in 67 minutes and he was 67.07.

I sat in the group behind Colin till he dropped out at halfway. I ran another couple of miles with the guys in the group and I felt so good I pushed on. I had a good spell from 15 to 20 miles, round the Docklands. I was checking the clock and I was 5-minute-miling.

The last 6 miles generally went well and I was still passing other people even when I was going through a couple of bad patches. They were strange. You feel OK and then. . . . Well, being your first marathon, you think, 'Is it the dreaded wall I've just hit?' You tend to panic but you recover. I passed a few who had really hit the wall, they were barely running.

There were big gaps ahead. One stretch of road, coming up to the Tower, I couldn't see anybody. I needed other runners to be with. Running on your own is a nightmare, especially if there's nobody in front. People in the crowd were shouting, 'Your brother's up ahead,' but I never saw him till I was kicking down The Mall. The tannoy was saying, 'And here's his brother . . .' and he turned round and gave me a shout.

But I was pleased with my run. A solid debut. A good performance. 2.15.25. Twenty-third.

Ian Hudspith's marathon tip
Don't be discouraged if you're not racing particularly well. If you've done the training, you'll be OK.

Mark Hudspith's marathon
They call the elite athletes over to the start about ten minutes beforehand. You have a bit of a chat with each other. When I did my first marathon I was terrified, about whether I could actually do it, at a good pace, but this year I was watching what was going on as an experienced marathon runner. Three of the lads from the club were doing their first: Ian, Terry and Billy. Their general demeanour the night before had suggested nervousness. They weren't as loud. Or cracking jokes.

I think I stood next to Ian. At that moment you've reached the point of no return. You've just got to get on with it. The last couple of minutes, you start concentrating, and then you're locked into it.

I was running in the second group. There was supposed to be a designated pacemaker to take us through to halfway in 65 minutes but he got carried away and the pace he was going at was more a 63-minute pace. He was up with the leaders when he should have been leading the second group. I had to make a decision not to go with the pace, and I let him go.

Fortunately, I ended up in quite a decent-sized group. All the main contenders, they didn't go either, so I found myself running with a lot of unexpected people, guys who hoped they were going to win the race. So I got quite a good ride till halfway. I was two minutes up on Ian.

Then I got dropped. It was a lapse of concentration. I reached a drink station and was looking for a bottle and when I looked up they were 20, 30 yards away and I never managed to claw them back. I was thinking, 'I'm going to have quite a long, lonely run now,' and it turned out like that, to be honest. It was hard work. I had to keep pushing myself, maintain a reasonable pace.

The headwind was getting stronger and stronger, but I still ran a decent race till 2 miles to go. It was the effort of running those 11 miles in the middle on my own. I had in my head at the start that I wanted to run a PB, which would have meant 2.12. And then you get towards the end and you realise that's not going to happen. I finished in 2.15.11.

I was 22nd, second Briton home behind Jon Brown, so it wasn't really a failure from that respect, just from my own personal point of view because I'd run seven marathons and before the race I was looking for a breakthrough into world class: 2.10.

It was quite tough, those last two miles. I probably had my best season leading up to the race and I certainly expected to run a PB, so I felt disappointed, I must say. But it passes with time. It's just part and parcel of running. You have a lot of those disappointments. There's nothing you can do about it. The best way you can get over it is to set yourself another target and chase that.

Mark Hudspith's marathon tip
Be dedicated in your training.

Helen Spriggs

Helen was running London for the third time, despite the challenge of being diabetic. She'd been diagnosed at 13, but she was determined not to let it control her life. She loved running marathons. She'd done New York twice. She knew it was always going to be difficult but she thought a sub-4.30

was within her reach and she put heart and soul into her training.

In early February she'd done the Puma 10k in Dewsbury, up north near her childhood home. The whole week before that race, she'd been really worried about it. She was convinced that she had to come in within 50 minutes. Everybody was going to be so fast, she thought. There'd be no one at her pace.

It was a really freezing day. Just before the race, she tested her glucose levels. Five times as high as normal. Probably because she was so nervous. But even though she knew the reason, that didn't make it any easier. When your levels were that high, it made you feel like you were running in treacle. No energy. You couldn't breathe.

It was such a hard slog and the first part was all uphill. She got to the top and just threw up. She *couldn't* finish last. There were people finishing and she wasn't even halfway. She did 1.08 in the end. Seven or so other runners behind her, so she wasn't last. But she was so mad with herself, so disappointed.

But she got changed and sat down and after a bit she thought, 'That was good experience for me, running with other people.' When you ran on your own, like she'd been doing, you went into yourself. After the marathon was over, she'd join a club. So gradually she came round to thinking that Puma 10k was a positive experience for her after all.

And it really made her commit herself to training. No longer would she let herself have a day off if she got tired. She got herself a rucksack that fastened round the waist so it didn't bounce around, and started running home from work.

Work had been busy, a bit of a hassle, and she'd been finding it stressful anyway. Running home from it was almost like running away from her unhappiness. She started looking forward to five-thirty coming around so she could escape from it. And that was another plus. In the past, she'd been coming home with all these work problems on her mind and straight away dump them all on her boyfriend, Nayim. But with running home, she'd gone over it, worked it out in her head already.

Through February the weather had been really cold but then she started noticing how one more minute every day it stayed light. Suddenly she was finding new routes, seeing spring come up all around her, noticing the littlest things. Things you wouldn't notice from behind the wheel of a car. Though running home was infecting her with a new kind of road rage: tourists, pedestrians, pelican crossings, traffic lights. Things like that, they really wound her up.

But she was starting to feel stronger. She'd go out and do a distance second time around, and she'd do it faster and better. She'd lost more than a stone and that made her feel good. She'd always really loved food, especially all the things diabetics shouldn't like anyway. Now she was looking at what she was eating to see which food achieved the best results for her running.

It was time-consuming, no doubt about that. Her fifth marathon in two years. Your whole life was geared up to it; friends, work, you were scheduling it all round running. You wanted it that way but you were conscious of how it dominated everything else. It became your life.

One weekend, out running, she saw someone wearing this fabulous T-shirt: RING IN SICK, it said. Monday. She rang work and had a day off. She did a long run instead. There were so many other runners. It felt like everyone in central London was training.

If she was out in the car and saw someone running, she'd feel guilty. Once, when the weather was really bad and she was stuck indoors staring out of the bedroom window at the rain chucking down, Nayim said to her, 'You've got all the gear, go.' It was so hard, but she did it. She took that first step out of the door. And once she got out there, she found

147

so many runners. Faces just like hers. She felt so lifted. Like she and the other runners were part of something bigger than all of them. Even though nothing was spoken. They were all working towards the same goal.

She was waiting to get her race number when she heard from a friend that someone they both knew had already received theirs. That day she came in after running from work thinking, 'I hope it's come, what if it hasn't? What if I haven't got a place after all?' But the envelope was there waiting for her. She opened it in the bath. She felt so emotional. Tears in her eyes, everything. She knew what she was going to be part of and she knew it was going to be good. The greatest day.

Helen Spriggs's marathon
Two weeks before London I ran the Docklands Half-Marathon. I tell you, I had a hell of a time. I was doing a documentary for the BBC, *My Big Day*, and I didn't quite realise how much time would be taken up. I was to film 80 per cent of it myself and had to learn all sorts of camera skills, so there was all this preparation and wondering how on earth was I going to make a documentary on marathon day.

I would run home from work with a camera on my shoulder, or on a hat or in my hand, and the BBC would be here and we'd play it back and I've have a shot of my nose or I didn't realise how badly my chest bounced. So two weeks before London I did the Docklands Half-Marathon as a trial run.

I had my bumbag full of glucose supplies, carbohydrates and blood-glucose testing equipment, and then I had tapes and batteries and God knows what for the camera. The Docklands starts with a lap of a running track and I'd just got round that in this sort of harness when I thought, 'There's no way I can do this.' That was after 400 metres. All I was thinking was that I wanted to do a good race and feel confident, and instead it was ending up just being a real kind of trial-and-error.

So I didn't do a good race. The BBC had people at various points to interview me and I finished in about $2\frac{1}{2}$ hours; it was a real hassle. Doing the documentary made me feel I just had something else to worry about as well as the marathon and my diabetes. I realised quite quickly I wasn't going to get 4.30. I was looking for 5.00. Or at the very latest 5.15.

I was much more dedicated in my training than I'd been at any other time in my life. A lot of effort had gone into it and I felt I deserved to get something out of it. I'd bored everyone at work, my friends, my family, my boyfriend Nayim, so this camera was like something I sneaked off to talk to who wasn't going to shout back and say, 'Shut up.'

But the nearer and nearer it came to the marathon I started to get all these doubts, and the positive feelings of a month before went out of the window. I forgot what I'd actually done. I felt it was like exams – yes, you *have* revised, you *have* worked hard. It was as though in those last few days I forgot all that and just wanted to cram.

I stopped running on the Thursday and started to feel, 'This is marathon time,' though I still had all these doubts. My parents came down for the weekend. On the Friday at work the Good Luck e-mails were coming through, and they got me a bottle of champagne.

The day before, I went to see them construct the finish line, which is a bit of a ritual. That visualisation that you're going to be there the next day. I had that finish line logged in my head. I thought, 'If I get struck down by lightning I'll crawl to that place, I will make it.' I'm stronger in my mind than in my body and in my legs. You have to have the mental strength to do the training.

And then, I don't know . . . I was conscious of having to

get a lot of rest but there was pressure with this document-ary. The time I had was taken up because we had to go and film the British Diabetic Association pasta party.

It was a nice enough evening. A lot of diabetic Americans came over to run: people I'd been speaking to on the internet, in particular someone who'd lacked a bit of confidence but had read what I'd written. And that made me feel proud: 'Wow! Changing someone's thoughts around.' I'd made it possible for them.

But those last few days I felt I was more active and stressed than I'd like to have been. The night before, I had all these pre-race worries going on: my diabetes, have I had enough carbohydrates, would I wake up? All that getting the kit ready, laying it out. I had all these different Puma kits and I was having to decide which one I felt confident in. I dreamed that I started the race wearing my flip-flops, and they kept coming off.

I woke up on Sunday morning with a really low blood-sugar level. It can drop to a level where you start to get symptoms like hitting the wall: you're weak, confused, hungry, disorien-tated, fearful, your heart's going. Straight away I thought, 'I hope I'm not going to suffer with this all day.' The more emphasis I put on a run, the more it happens. That kind of anticipation can raise your level or can make it hit the floor.

I took a fast-acting glucose tab and a longer-acting carbohydrate. I got all geared up and went with my dad to the start. It was really good to be with my dad. In the last few months he's taken up running. I think he's tempted to do a marathon but he won't say it. I'll say, 'Yeah, I'll do it,' and not really think about it. But my dad likes to map it all out. He's a lot more cautious. I just want to say to him, 'Do it.'

Two hours before a race I take my insulin. It's a fifth of what I would normally take because exercise makes you use insulin far more efficiently. It's all about getting that balance; you need enough insulin to turn food into energy.

I had a sandwich of banana mixed with honey on granary bread. There were wine gums, fruit pastilles, rice crispie bars and orange drinks in my bumbag. It's not really a bumbag, it's a great, fitted belt thing which disperses the weight evenly around you. I'd lost weight but I was carrying more weight in the bag, so it evened out.

You sometimes wish you didn't have to do it, carry all this extra stuff. I wasn't worrying about blisters, or all the other kinds of things people normally worry about; my main concern was that I'd got enough things for my diabetes. I had to have friends positioned along the course who could hand out extra supplies. I run with my glucometer in my hand like a stopwatch.

It took me twelve minutes to get over the start. It was fun. I carried the camera for the first mile, then handed it over to someone and picked it up again at 5. I did the first 6 miles within the hour. I loved it, those first 6, 7, 8 miles.

Then I started to get into problems. Sweating, tiredness. I ignored it, thinking, 'It's just because I'm running,' but when I did a test on my glucometer I started to realise things weren't going as well as I wanted. I felt weak; I kept drinking juice but that didn't seem to be enough. I passed Tower Bridge. My mum was there. 'How are things going?' she asked.

'It's not gonna get me. It's not gonna get control.'

But as I got into Docklands things started to go wrong and I began to feel quite scared. When you're running, you might be taking glucose in but you're using it very quickly as well. It's like running a bath when the tap's on and the water's running down the plughole at the same time.

I really felt, 'Ach, I can't eat anything, not when I'm running.' I was taking on so much fluid it was like force-feeding myself. That was soul-destroying, realising that unless I gave myself time out I was not going to make it.

I thought, 'What am I doing?' You ask yourself this quite a

lot during a marathon, but if I collapsed it would be off to hospital for me, and I thought it wasn't worth risking that. And I started thinking of the camera, and the message I wanted to give. So I started walking.

I was well behind my schedule anyway. Between 17 and 18 miles was the worst part. I felt really disappointed in myself. I started to hate my diabetes. Defeated by something I wanted to defeat. Wallowing in a bit of self-pity. And I was thinking of my job, working with teenagers with diabetes, giving them challenges, showing them how to accept it; I thought, 'I'm putting all these kids through it, and here I am, like this.' I felt ashamed.

I thought, 'God, am I using diabetes as a scapegoat? What a stupid thought! How can I go back into work and say I had a really bad marathon because of my diabetes?'

Living with diabetes, sometimes you can question it. 'Have I really got it?' Because you feel so on top of the world. At other times it can shock you into reality. You *have* got something wrong with you.

I wanted people to understand what I'd gone through. I haven't got a limb missing. You can't see that my pancreas has packed up. Sometimes with that invisible disability people can't understand the fear and the worry and the force-feeding and the loss of energy. But the kids, if they don't get a boyfriend, if they fail their exams, they blame the diabetes, and through the newsletter I produce and the events I organise I'm saying to them, 'Don't do that.' Now I was thinking, 'I wonder if people will think I'm doing exactly that?'

Michelle Harris was my childhood friend. She died in July 1997, in a car crash. She was 23. I know this is going to sound corny, but at that moment I started thinking about her and my levels started to rise.

I really was thinking about her. I was in tears. I thought,

'Come on, you've been with me in training.' I thought about all the mischief she used to get up to. I was talking aloud to her. 'Come on, Michelle, take me home!' She was going to be like my last bit of wind that took me through that home straight.

It's an emotional rollercoaster. After those 20 miles, those feelings of wanting to give up, you know there's no going back. You become very . . . withdrawn. However much I loved that crowd at one point, I hated it the next. I got sick of hearing them shout, 'Helen!' It was like a massive invasion of your space, your privacy.

And then I went totally back to visualising. 'I've just started running now. This is my Sunday route home.' You're playing mind games. Tricking your body into thinking you're fresh.

Along that last stretch, it was going into the unknown because each marathon is a different journey. In that last bit you feel the loneliest you'll ever feel. Even though there's all those runners, all those people lining the streets, friends rooting for you and your gran watching it on the telly in Scunthorpe, there's only you who can do it in the end.

Through the last 5 miles and along the Embankment, I definitely wanted to vomit. Believe me. All that stuff I'd had to take, it was lying on me, I was just really wanting to be sick. I really felt it, that last stretch. Soon as I could see Big Ben, my eyes were on it all the time. Speeding up as well because I was trying to make the best of it. I went for it. I overtook some poor souls on their last legs. 5.37.

After I crossed the finish line and got my medal, I did the biggest projectile vomit. I was proud of it. I was green, I was white and once I'd got it over with I was fine again. My mum and dad were right at the finish and I just got hold of my mum and sobbed my heart out and she did too. All those things you've been running with for hours; at last you can tell someone.

At first I was ashamed, disappointed. I didn't want to talk about how I'd done the marathon. 'God, Helen, it was your fifth marathon, what were you doing?' I felt bitter about the whole thing. They were all patting me on the back and I couldn't understand why.

It was only later that I thought, 'I've done five marathons, what an achievement.' It's not just passing the finish line; it's dealing with all the things that are thrown at you in those 26 miles. That pain. You kind of get a bit of pleasure out of it. A kind of glorying in it, in a sense. Your war wounds.

On the Tuesday I had to get my trainers on and go out. Legs like lead weights. But then on the Monday, a week after the marathon, I said to myself, 'Right. Back into training for New York.'

Helen Spriggs's marathon tip
To run 26 miles, you have to draw on qualities you never knew you had to push you through.

Kev Wood

When he got the chance of a London place, Kev didn't make the decision to run it lightly. He'd been there already, eleven years back, done a respectable time, gone on to other things; maybe once was enough. In all honesty, he had mixed feelings about the event. It certainly wasn't his favourite.

He was aiming at breaking three hours but around the beginning of February he wasn't wonderfully confident. As a consequence of the extra training he'd been putting in, he had more colds and flu that winter than ever before. He had flu over the Christmas holiday and took days to recover from that. He spoke to his former coach and they were chatting away and the coach was a little bit gloomy: 'You'd have hoped for higher mileage by now.'

So that motivated Kev. He was going to see if he could still break three. That weekend he ran to the bridge at Picketts Lock and turned round: 22 miles. After that, he just settled into training really. He ran the Essex 20 on Valentine's Day and did 2.12.31 and then he kept on and had a very effective week in Portugal, spring training. In the rest of his life there was no great pressure. It was quite a luxury and an indulgence to go off spring training for a week. Not everyone could afford that, or agree it with a partner.

He was focused on his goal, yeah, but he was cagey about it. He didn't tell many people. He really didn't want to set himself up to fail, to be judged. Come 18 April, he really didn't know what would happen.

Kev Wood's marathon
Registration's always very pleasant. I'd taken Thursday morning off work and I was able to spend a couple of hours at the London Arena, going round the stalls. I got some new racing shoes for the future, some Mizuno ones, I thought I'd give them a go. The most pleasant thing was talking to a few people, both friends and clubmates, and Mike Gratton from the *Runner's World* training camp, and Keith Anderson, the very fast veteran who works for Adidas, he knows a mutual friend so I introduced myself to him. The point of this is not to say I was hobnobbing with all these famous runners but just to say how approachable they are. I mean, I suppose they were there to sell things, but there was no pressure.

I was aware of getting plenty of rest and eating the right things leading up to the race. I wasn't very excited by it, actually. I was viewing it as a chore, something I had to go and do. I didn't want to build it up into a great event. I was surprised to have a start off Shooter's Hill rather than Greenwich Park because I am a vet and they usually start from the park. I was really pleased to get Shooter's Hill, actually, because it's a faster start. I was lucky as well, I got into the first pen, which put me just behind the elite and AAAs people. I got into the pen with about 25 minutes to go and it only took me 16 seconds to cross the line. It took one of the *Runner's World* Team in Training sub-three people three or four minutes.

I'd got a very clear mile split that I was aiming at. I had 6.40 in mind. Conventional coaching theory suggests that the best times are achieved when runners run either even miles splits, or when suitably prepared runners run the second half faster than the first. But I adopted a strategy where I was trying to run just within the split so I could get some time in the bank for the later stages when I would be justified in feeling I wouldn't be able to sustain 6.40. I ran 6.25–6.40 for as long as I could. I was very pleased with anything under 6.40. I didn't go for anything like 6.10s. I used a stopwatch.

To be honest I can't say I enjoyed the race, really. I felt very focused, very attuned towards the task. I enjoyed running the half mile at the bottom of my street. It felt very much like home territory. Just up the road from it was the 10k marker and it was really satisfying to go under there in just under 40 minutes because for years I'd struggled to break 40 and hadn't, and it was really good to do that in the context of the race and feel comfortable.

There was a lot of support from clubmates and friends all along the course. It was really good all the way round. I felt very positive about that. I was very much tied in to the task and once again experience or perhaps knowledge helped; when I got to around 21 miles I started to feel pretty rough but I knew what that was about really – the physiological nutritional change when your body starts to burn fat. I knew that would pass if I kept going.

I'd gone the other side of the 6.40s by then. At that stage I dropped off quite a bit but I did pull back from it. I'm a great believer in psychological tricks and things to boost your confidence because much of it is to do with that kind of approach. I had this strategy that every mile in the later stage of the race I'd think about running economically and with good form and I'd draw strength from that. Of course, it's much easier to do that if you've got a little time in hand and you're not behind the schedule you set for yourself.

I don't think about the other runners. No. No. No. I think there was only one stage where I noticed somebody from another club, slightly ahead of me – I was keeping the same margin, we maintained the same distance. The one thing which amused me – irritated me at the time – was that going towards Big Ben I was overtaken by someone wearing fancy dress. Batman. I'd just heard the course commentator say, 'And here's the first runner in fancy dress.' I know that many good runners faster than me run in fancy dress, but it was good to hear that Batman was the first and that there weren't any more closing on me.

Anyway, Batman overtook me but I kept going. I knew things were pretty nip and tuck to beat three hours. In February when I had some sort of virus I was walking along Birdcage Walk and I thought, 'There's a slight slope here. Oh dear. I shouldn't have walked along here because after 25 miles it'll be at the back of my mind.' But I told myself to shut up and not be so silly, it wasn't as if it was the North Face of the Eiger.

And then it was just a matter of checking the watch and trying to get round the corner into the Mall in under three hours. Which I did. I did 2.59.27.

The 33 seconds which separated me from the three-hour mark are just incredibly precious and worth their weight in gold. Had I even done three hours dead I would have been left with something to achieve. My ambivalence towards this marathon has been appalling. I now don't have to do it again and I can try and achieve other goals if I want. I've been released.

Kev Wood's marathon tip
Get out and do some long runs by yourself. It toughens you up mentally.

Flo Gibson

It was going to be Flo's third London. Her first ever was a sub-six – she'd been proud of herself just for finishing. The next year, 1998, even though she found running hard she'd put in extra training. She'd done a 4.50, knocking 34 minutes off her time. This year she was going to work even harder. She was going for a sub-4.30.

In February she did the Benfleet 15 and it was really, really windy. Her partner Bob ran it as well, and he hadn't been doing any training so she wasn't expecting to go anywhere very fast. In fact, she hadn't been going to bother at all, but Alan Reynolds from her club was doing it and he said, 'I'll run it with you. I'm not running for a time.'

They ended up walking most of it because of the weather. Her jacket was flapping and filling up with air; you just couldn't move forward. Oh, it was awful, that day, she thought it was never going to end. Took about three hours. Her eyes were streaming from about 7 miles. When they got to that bit when they were running on the downs, it was really boggy. They decided to tiptoe on the dry bits, but there weren't any dry bits. She was screeching with laughter because she could hear all this effing and blinding from Bob in front of her. 'Oh, fuckin' 'ell,' he kept going. She just couldn't take the race seriously any more. This woman she saw in the toilet afterwards said to her, 'I knew what was coming up was going to be horrible because I was behind you, I could hear you laughing.'

Most Sundays after that, she did the club long run. The River Lea towpath towards Pickett's Lock and back, or two circuits of Woolwich and Barking High Street. Fourteen miles, then 16, 18, a couple of 20s. One Sunday, she and a woman friend were running past an old gypsy encampment by the river when they got chased by a couple of guys who'd been sleeping rough. The guys were out of condition, they'd been up all night drinking by the look of them, but one of them was young, he tracked them almost a mile, even when they speeded up. Then they caught up with Bob and the guy just vanished. They joked about it afterwards, said now they'd discovered the secret of how to run 7-minute miles. But it had been scary.

Around that time her back started to hurt and she had one week of feeling really exhausted, pound, pound, pound on the roads and then having to stand for long hours working the equipment for her ironing service. But that's the way it always was in March. You just had a couple of massages and a couple of weeks easy. You just got on with it. Then two weeks before London, she ran a personal best of 2.03 in the Docklands Half-Marathon. She wasn't making any promises, but sub-4.30 was still within her sights. She also had a private goal, which she hadn't intended letting on to anyone. Particularly Bob.

Flo Gibson's marathon

It was just a personal thing, the sub-4.30, a challenge against myself. Actually, I was trying to beat Bob! You can't put that down. Oh all right, but you know this'll be divorce.

We met up with the rest of the club at Island Gardens like we always do. My son Jay took us there and took lots of photos. Bob buzzing? Don't make me laugh. When's Bob ever buzzing? He was just looking to finish because he hadn't put the training in. He's got natural stamina. If he put the training in, I wouldn't stand a chance.

Bob and I were running together at first, with Jerome,

another clubmate. We'd done 6 miles when Bob said, 'Slow down, you're going too fast.' But I was just running at a steady pace in front of them.

How I look at it is, the first half of the race is across the water and when I get over Tower Bridge I'm on home ground again. So going down The Highway for the first time Bob and Jerome overtook me and I just shut my mind off, I knew I'd got to run my own race, steady pace.

I started looking out for people I knew, Jay and the club members who weren't running, and my mum in Poplar. I saw Marie from down the club in Poplar High Street, outside the pub. On the Isle of Dogs I saw one of my sisters. She just jumped out of the crowd: 'Go, Flo, go!' Gives you a bit of a boost. Then I saw my masseur's dad, giving me a shout out of the blue.

I met some people I'd met on other runs. A fella who'd done the Docklands. In the Docklands he'd said to me, 'People say I must be mad to do this.' So I met him again in the London and he said, 'I definitely must be mad.'

'I think we all are,' I said.

I started getting tired about 16 miles. I was feeling it then, but I shut my mind off, pretended I was doing a Tuesday session down the track. When I came back down The Highway I saw one of my customers for the ironing. My friend Carol is usually at the 24-mile mark but she wasn't there this year, or maybe I missed her. When Big Ben was in sight it seemed so near and yet you've got so long still to get there. Then just turning the corner by the Houses of Parliament someone tripped me, but he caught me. I thought I was going to go. I felt so weak at the time, I wouldn't have been able to save myself.

I just shut off and imagined. Just putting one foot in front of the other in the end. I didn't think I had a sprint in me, but then I saw the clock and it said 4.38 and I just wanted to get there before it said 4.39. And I did manage a sprint and that made me feel really great, getting there before it said 4.39.

At the end I just felt relieved and pleased that I'd finished, but so weak. When someone handed me a bottle of water I couldn't take the lid off, and when I went to get my baggage it felt like a ton. I don't like crowds, but the baggage area was gridlocked with people. I just wanted to put my bag down, and get dressed and find Bob.

I went to a changing hut and it was the only place where there was space. A woman in there had spread her tinfoil blanket out and was sitting on it eating all the stuff from her goody bag, like a little picnic. I really wanted to do that but at the same time I just wanted to find Bob so I got dressed and went back outside into the crowd.

Eventually I got over to meeting place E for East End Road Runners. I waited for Bob and he came over and I didn't know what time he'd done. It was 4.41. All the time I'd thought he was in front but I must have passed him on the Isle of Dogs. He said he was pleased for me, but I felt I had to be careful. He's sensitive, Bob.

I was starving. I got an extra sandwich in case Bob hadn't picked one up because you always get something for the men to eat. But he didn't want it so I ate it. 'The vitamins, they're quite nice,' he said. 'Fizzy.' So I popped one in my mouth and I was foaming. Because you're meant to take them in water, aren't you?

We'd all arranged to meet up at a pub boat on the Embankment, which was nice because usually you just go away on your own afterwards. But halfway through the second drink everyone looked cold, tired and miserable, wanting to be home in the bath and warmed up again.

I was happy with my time and I wasn't. By my watch I'd done 4.28 because I lost ten minutes getting over the start, but I would have felt better if I'd done 4.28 on that clock. It's a personal thing. I was pleased but I would have been more pleased if I'd done it in 4.30.

Looking back on it, I probably enjoyed the training, getting up on Sunday to do the long runs, because otherwise you'd only be sitting around. But it's the wear and tear on your body that takes it out of you, all the bad backs and the going to the osteopath. When I did my first marathon, I remember running along the Embankment when they had music on and I got really emotional. I didn't cry, but I wanted to. Nothing's been as good as that first one. It's like going back to the same party, isn't it?

I was going to make this the last year but if I'm going to finish I'm going to finish on the Millennium. My brother-in-law says to me, 'Once you've done it, you don't have to do it again.' People who don't run always think that – you've proved your point, you can just hang your shoes up.

But you can't hang your shoes up, you'd get as fat as a pig, for a start. It's a matter of *having* to keep on now. Oh, you always say you're going to finish soon but you never do.

I saw this old lady running it and I want to be like that. Running when I'm old. Someone said to me, 'But aren't you worried something'll happen to you?' And I just had to laugh because, well, if you're old something *is* going to happen to you, isn't it? You might as well keep running till it does.

Flo Gibson's marathon tip
Be positive and tell yourself you can do it.

Tony Evans

After a long-term addiction to alcohol and cocaine an accident left Tony with a serious brain injury two years back. Once he recovered consciousness he was forced to relearn how to walk and talk. He vowed to celebrate his recovery by running the London Marathon. His early training had gone well and he had successfully completed an 18-mile run with his training partner and keyworker at Rehab UK, Matthew Tatton.

Matthew had found out all about him. They weren't close like mates, but they'd got this relationship now; Tony had done the long runs with him, met his wife. He was a nice man, without a doubt. In the very early stages of training they'd done a 5-mile race with a lot of hills together. Tony had wanted to see if his balance would be all right, because that was one of the things he'd been worried about. Another worry was that he didn't like people around him, and it would have been pointless going in for a marathon if he really couldn't stand the crowds. But the race had been a good test. He'd enjoyed it.

Then, four weeks before the start, he'd done all the ligaments in his left knee. He'd been working out in the gym and he just felt them tear. It didn't hurt. He'd just thought, 'Strange . . .' But it had meant stopping training. He'd started getting really, really worried; worried that he wouldn't be able to do it.

Of all the times for his knee to have gone. Matthew said he could end up doing it some really bad damage if he went through with the marathon. Tony had already had so many doubts. One day he'd be fine with people around him, the next day he'd be in a panic. And he'd had all the anxieties about his balance and his mental state, times when he'd thought, 'I'm never going to be able to do it.'

And with his knee going as well, he'd been gutted. But he wasn't going to give up. The thought of him not running, at least not *trying* to run it, just never crossed his mind. Whatever happened, he was going to give it a really good go.

Tony Evans's marathon

I'd been out and bought a professional knee brace. I strapped it on so tight it was like being in a vice. I knew my mentality was right, my balance was OK, but beyond a

163

shadow of a doubt my knee was going to play up. It was on my mind all the week leading up to the start, and it was on my mind when I was standing on the start line. Just the one question: 'When's it going to go?'

My cousin in Portugal wanted me to run with a phone so he could speak to me before the start, so I'd got this phone with a mouthpiece. I got to Greenwich Park, put my St George's flag on, and straightaway the phone rang; it was my cousin. We started running and there were people phoning me up all the way along. I quite liked it but once I'd got a sweat on and I was 10 miles into the race I got so annoyed I thought I was going to throw the thing into the road. Then I saw my wife Sam and my boys so I ran over and said, 'This is going to do my head in,' and gave it to them.

I was running with Matthew and for 18 miles I was fine, coasting. We were hoping for a 4.00 or 4.15 finish and were bang on target. But at about 19 miles I got into an ambulance, took the strapping off and my knee swelled into a balloon before my eyes.

They put ice on it and strapped it up again and I ran as far as the next ambulance. I said to Matthew, 'Look, you just carry on running and I'll do the best I can.'

Of course, he said, 'No, no. We finish together.' So we had an argument. But in the end he ran on.

Once he'd gone I felt relieved. I knew he was fine. I only had to worry about myself. I got to the 20-mile mark and the next ambulance and said, 'Should I walk it?' and the St John attendant said, 'You should think about stopping.' So I started walking. The last 6 miles felt like a hundred. If I'd laid down and got physio I'd have never got up.

Sam, my wife, had been waiting further along the route. She knew something was wrong because I hadn't come past her and when I got to that narrow little street just after The Highway she came running up with the boys.

I said, 'I'm not going to make it. My knee's gone.'

So she walked with me. Held my hand for the last 4 miles. With my boys. We all plodded along. My Auntie Avril was at 24 miles, she started crying when she seen me walking with Sam and limping, and my Auntie Dink was with her and she started crying, and when we walked down Birdcage Walk the atmosphere and the support I got from everyone there made it even more touching. But it was the support I got from her. Sam. That was the big thing. When the question was, would I walk again? was I going to be retarded? And 20 months later there was me and her walking down Birdcage Walk together.

Afterwards I thought to myself, 'I finished even though I had a bad knee. I still had the determination.' But the bottom line is, when the medal was put round my neck I didn't feel the euphoria I thought I would. There was something missing. I'd done the training, I was confident. At the 18-mile marker we were bang on time for four hours. I was focused. It could have been 36 miles for all I cared. I had inside me the ability and fitness to run it from start to finish but I couldn't because my knee had said, 'Hello! You're not running any more,' and there was nothing I could do.

I hadn't achieved what I'd wanted to achieve. That's what gives me the incentive to do it again next year. I want to run it from start to finish without the help of my wife. Plus I've got to beat the time. I know it's there.

Two days after the marathon I went up to Northwick Park Hospital where I'd been treated after the accident, and I recognised the surgeon who'd operated on me. I said, 'D'you remember me?'

He said, 'Oh yes, you're that nutty Chelsea fan who kept throwing himself off the bed.'

I said, 'D'you remember I told you I was going to run the London Marathon?' and I put my medal in his hand.

He took me along to his ward, called all the nurses round,

got my head down and showed them my scar. He said, 'This was the guy we thought would never walk again. This is what makes my job worthwhile.' And that felt better than the moment when I finished.

I've got to say it took me three days to come down after the marathon. First two days I was hyper. Jumping around shouting, 'I'm all right, I'm all right!' On the third day I was walking like John Wayne. I didn't mind. Twenty months back I'd been told I might never walk, talk, communicate, use my limbs again. I am now able to stand and look normal. I've given a couple of speeches in front of politicians and I've run a marathon. A lot of people *without* a brain injury couldn't do that.

Tony Evans's marathon tip
It's not over till it's over.

Karen Hutchings

Karen had been particularly busy in her job at Swissair all through January and February and on top of that she and her partner John had spent three weeks skiing. Consequently she had let her training lapse and it wasn't till March that she decided to have a go at London anyway. Then she plunged into intensive training.

The longest run she did was 15 miles two weeks before the race, whereas normally she'd have done a 21-miler three weeks before. It was mega-busy at work, so often instead of running she'd go to the gym, because that didn't close till ten-thirty. Or if she could get away from work by seven she would run home to Barking from Leicester Square. Eleven or twelve miles, taking in the Embankment, the Thames, Docklands, so it was a nice run all the way till she hit the A13. That was one long, gloomy, dark, straight road. Dirty as well.

The best thing was that John had decided to do London as well, so they were pushing out together. The only thing was that he worked nights, so he'd be training during the day. She missed training with him, even when he whinged about his injuries all the time or when he called her a pain in the arse. They understood each other's moods, and supported each other.

Karen Hutchings's marathon

I never got worried about actually running the marathon. It wasn't like the pressure of two years back when I'd done a lot of training and was going for a time. When we were lining up at the start, waiting for the hooter to go, I got the usual butterflies but really I was just running to get round.

The whole of our running club met at Island Gardens, like they always do, to walk along Greenwich Foot Tunnel to the start. It didn't feel like a whole year had passed. It had gone so quickly. But anyway, I don't look back that much. I was already thinking about New York in November, then Florida 2000. Why look back when you can look forward to whatever you've got coming later on? Like I've said, you're only here once, so make the most of it. When I met my now ex-husband I was 20. We just grew apart. As soon as John and I met I knew life could be different, so I went for it. And it's been perfect.

I was supposed to be in Red Start but I went to Blue because John was going from there. They have a baggage lorry for people with Red numbers at Blue start. Not many people know that! Blue Start is so much better, though it still took John and me nearly ten minutes to get over the line, and after that the pace was still fairly slow. But time didn't matter.

John and I talked and ran at the same time. I just decided that whenever I saw anyone I knew I'd stop and talk, give myself a breather, not just wave and run past. I saw one of my clients at 5 miles – he ran past me, which was an interesting experience. Then at 14 miles we saw the first East End Road Runners support group, and a mile further on my mum and dad were waiting with bananas and chocolate for John. He gets so hungry when he runs. Mum had set out the bananas and chocolate by the railings – she felt dreadful because people had been running past asking for the bananas and she couldn't hand them out because she was saving them for John. Then he didn't want them, only the chocolate, so she felt even worse.

As soon as I saw Mum and Dad it started to kick into me that this was going to be difficult, that I hadn't done the training. I knew I had Docklands and the Isle of Dogs ahead, and they're so damn quiet. John had all these aches and pains as usual but, I think because he'd been a boxer, he was able to shut them out.

I got to 17 miles and I had to have a little walk. I said to him, 'Go on,' but he wouldn't leave me. Then we hit the Isle of Dogs and I was surprised because there were a hell of a lot more spectators than I'd thought, and it was packed with runners as well. My natural running speed was so much quicker than the others around me, so that when I started running again after having my little walk the sheer numbers of people made it difficult to overtake.

By 18 miles, because of all the dodging and weaving I was doing, I could feel the blisters kicking in because having missed so much training my feet weren't hardened. The worst was on the ball of my foot, and I had two underneath my toenails. But I got a boost at 19 miles because I happened to see one of my clients in the crowd. He didn't recognise me in shorts, as opposed to business attire. I ran up to him and said, 'George! How are you?' And he said, 'Karen, you don't look so good.'

And I must say that after 19 miles, it was the thought of all the friends I was going to see that kept me hanging on. We were dead lucky at 21 miles because John's brother Barry caught us unexpectedly, and gave us a can of Red Bull to share. He was on the corner, just as you come back onto The Highway. It was so brilliant to see him, and then the second of the East End Road Runners support groups at 22 miles. I stopped and nattered till my clubmate Maggie said, 'What are you doing standing here talking to us? Get on and finish.'

My friend Sally was giving out water at the drinks station on the City side of the Embankment, so I was hanging on for her. Then I caught up another clubmate who was running. I must say that the last time I'd been on a training run with him, he'd been rather patronising, asking me if I was OK afterwards. I mean, *me*, who'd run more than a dozen marathons when he was a veteran of one! So it gave me great pleasure to say, 'Are you OK?' as I passed him.

I knew Mum and Dad and a lot of friends would be on the Embankment. I saw them all there and they took their photos. I was not feeling my best, but I was still running. Then at 25 miles I turned to John and said, 'I've got to walk.' He put his arms round me and gave me a kiss. I caught sight of two girls watching us. One said to the other, 'Oh, isn't it sweet?' Their eyes were welling up. Well, you do well up at the London Marathon, don't you? I always do, anyway.

John and I came round the corner at Westminster Bridge and into Birdcage Walk. I saw one of my best friends there. She'd been a bridesmaid at my wedding. We both gave her a big, sweaty kiss and then carried on towards the end.

We finished and we got our medals. We had the obligatory embrace. After that we went to meet parents, friends, everybody from the club on the *Tattershall Castle* pub boat where we always do. We had a beer or two. And that was that.

We did 4.10. The only thing was that John was disappointed, because he reckoned that if we hadn't stopped so often we would have done sub-four. But I knew that next year we might be going for a time, and if so I won't be able to stop and talk and say thanks to all my people. So I wanted to do it just the once.

Karen Hutchings's marathon tip
Find people to train with. Don't do it on your own.

Tushar Patel

After missing out narrowly on his target of tenth place in his last two London marathons, Tushar was hoping for a personal best and a top five finish in the wheelchair race. The build-up coincided with the beginning of the wheelchair racing season. He had a major race on 14 March, the road-race championships in Portsmouth. He'd been pretty nervous, panicking at the start. Just didn't do as well as he should have done, in consequence. The panic totally threw him, he couldn't concentrate on what he wanted to do. He was looking at the other athletes, choosing targets, when he should have been concentrating. He knew who was in front of him and who he wanted to beat and he thought, 'I'm going to get in there.' And while he was doing all that he totally lost his focus.

He'd been training with his new coach, Jenny Arche. She'd been doing well with him. The best thing was that she took it positively. Jenny said to him, 'It's good that they don't know what you can do and that they think you're still on the low level. Now you can concentrate on doing well in London.' But he was going to have to learn how to be calm on the start line.

Tushar Patel's marathon
I was getting a bit nervous again. I tried to keep myself calm and did all sorts of arm tricks, just warming up really. I saw the camera on me and it took the focus off the race. It was

good, it kept me calm and when it started I just shot off without thinking anything.

I didn't want to beat anyone specific. I knew if I got in the top five I'd beat my targets. So it was about beating my time and place. I was aware of the course at certain points, like when it came to a slow push at Tower Bridge because of the hill, and because it was packed with spectators. The noise was so big I actually raised my arm.

For me, the last 3 to 4 miles were really hard. I was worn out at 18. Constant pushing at high pace. Normally I'd been keeping that up for 10, and here I was keeping it up almost twice as long. But the Whizz-Kidz support team was at Marsh Wall, 30-odd kids making a big noise; that lifted me.

The next time I looked at my clock it was 21–22 miles. I started feeling worn out then but I knew I had to keep it up because once you drop off from the pack it's really hard on your own. With the pack, you're doing 4-minute miles, and if you're on your own it's more like 6 or 7. You can't get yourself to move again; everything's dying out. It happened to me last year when I crashed at 3 miles. I tried to get back but at 20–21 it was so hard.

The last 5 miles went past in a snap of the fingers. I hung on till the finish. I knew the bend. In the finishing stretch I started sprinting but after fifteen metres I was into the finish line. Head to head the last two or three metres. I just couldn't do it, I just couldn't make the first five. But I knew I'd done such a good time. 1.48.20. My personal best.

At that point I had it in my mind that I'd come seventh, because the person I was working with took me at the finish. Then when I met my uncle and the Whizz-Kidz support team I found that I was sixth. Had I known I was going to come sixth – and I was only two seconds behind that guy – it would have boosted me, I would have worked that much harder for fifth. I guess I just lost sight of the people in front of me.

I think I got pleased too quickly. I knew before I'd finished that I'd done a good time and that took my head off it. But I was very happy. For the last two years I've been trying to get in the top ten and missing out by seconds, and now I've got in four or five places higher. But there was still a little bit of regret.

Usually when I come away from a race and haven't achieved targets I want, I tend to sleep for the rest of the day, but that day I couldn't sleep till midnight; the PB just gave me that little boost of energy. I went to my uncle's house and played with my nephew instead.

I had blisters on my fingers. I noticed them when I got home, when I took my gloves off and had a shower. A big piece of skin came off. I'd felt some pain but there had been so much going on I didn't take any notice.

I felt it the next day, though. I felt my shoulders had been stretched. I felt a bit broader-shouldered. I wasn't in the mood for working. The aura was still around me. I went to college but came home early. I was so looking forward to going to training that evening to tell Jenny, my coach, about it but she knew already. Then I started thinking about my next target.

Tushar Patel's marathon tip
If you wish, you can. That's what I believe in.

Caroline Taraskevics

It all started in the summer of 1998. Her 40th birthday was coming up and she decided to celebrate it by getting fit. She was tall and slim, with a real runner's physique, but set against that were her wild teenage years and her past life in the rock industry with all the drug abuse. Since then she'd had some therapy, run her own business and lived happily in the West Country with her second husband, raising four kids. But there were still issues left to resolve. She wanted to feel good about her body, in a way she never had. She hoped running would enable her to do that. And she wanted to run this, her first marathon, in memory of her father.

Leslie Crowther had been a famous entertainer; Caroline was born on tour, in Edinburgh. A few years back he'd been in a terrible car crash, and died as a result of his brain injuries. Caroline got a place on the *Daily Telegraph* charity team, which was raising funds for the British Brain and Spine Foundation.

What she really loved about running was that you just needed a pair of shoes. That was all. You didn't need equipment. You could do it any time you liked. You weren't competing against anyone except yourself. One day she said to her husband, David, 'Running is part of my life now.' And he said, 'Oh God! I want a divorce!'

He'd go running with her but he'd feel terribly self-conscious. It was hard for him because she was getting to be a lot fitter than him. Not stronger, but fitter. Maybe it was a machismo thing. He had a problem with couples exercising together, yet he'd play tennis with her three times a day if she'd asked. He saw running as exercise, tennis as sport. Running was geeky, tennis was cool.

But she was growing to love almost everything about running. *Almost* everything. She was a rules girl, she was following the London Marathon Improvers schedule, but she'd had to do an awful lot of the training in West Country snow. One of the Sunday long runs was the worst in her life. It was really cold and it snowed almost the entire time she was running.

The worst part was that her feet got soaked almost immediately – and it was a $2\frac{1}{2}$ hour run. She had cold, wet feet for $2\frac{1}{2}$ hours. The wind was driving snow into her face.

She had a rainproof jacket on, and it was rubbing around her neck, and she'd put on tracksuit trousers which was a mistake because they got stuck and they flapped and they made it hard for her legs to move forward, and she swore and she muttered the whole way. Bloody snow, bloody God, bloody weather. She just felt so relieved when she got home.

She thought that was going to turn out to be the low point of her training, but then in March she got a ligament injury. She'd done one long run much longer than she was supposed to do it; instead of one-and-a-half hours she did two. She actually ran with the injury killing her for three more sessions, thinking she'd get over it. So she made it far worse and ended up not being able to run for two weeks.

She was in such a panic. She couldn't run at all. But someone gave her the name of the lady who looked after the Bath rugby team, and she had some really great physio. She also found a superb osteopath in Box, within hobbling distance from where she lived. So that was March – fretting about not running, and spending a lot of money on treatment.

The pain from the injury was horrendous. End of the world time. She fluctuated. She was new to intense exercise, she hadn't had to deal with injuries before, or work through them. She'd never had a deadline before. The worst thing was not knowing whether she was going to be better in time to perform. The physio and the osteopath were both saying that it was going to take two weeks, and that she wasn't going to lose an incredible amount of fitness, but she couldn't seem to get the doubts out of her mind. How long was it really going to keep her off? How should she start working again? It was all unknown. One minute she was saying, 'OK, I'm just going to walk round the marathon.' Then it was, 'No, it's going to be fine.' Then it was, 'I'm going to go out running tomorrow, whatever.'

Members of her family were bandying around words like 'obsessed'. But that was the kind of way she approached things. When she was a little girl, her grandfather had said to her, 'If a job's worth doing, it's worth doing well.' She'd never believed in going at things half-baked, and she wasn't going to start now.

Caroline Taraskevics's marathon

On the Monday before the race I'd had one great nightmare, a total marathon anxiety dream. I was running round the marathon course and we went past this castle which was owned by the Medici family. This woman came out and said, 'You've made your appointment to go round the castle and it's *now*.' And I felt I had to go in, and I was running round the castle looking at my watch. My daughter Kathleen said, 'Mum, I've found this doorway, and we can get out now.'

We looked out and the marathon was going on behind a barbed-wire fence. Kathleen said, 'It's OK, Mum, I can show you how to vault over it.' Then she got snagged and caught up in the wire, and was covered in blood. And then I woke up.

The day before the race, I met up with my younger brother Nicholas, who was also taking part. It was early evening and we had a phenomenally huge meal. I was completely stuffed.

Nicholas had far worse pre-race jitters than I had; he'd had panic attacks at work and hadn't been able to sleep that week, but I felt extraordinarily calm. I'd done everything I could do now. In fact I was *peculiarly* calm. I kept thinking, 'Why am I feeling like this, why aren't I feeling something else?'

When we went back to the hotel, I put my running gear on and my husband David took a photograph, and then, second by second, I went through my timetable for the morning. I phoned room service to organise some scrambled egg on toast to be brought to me at six a.m. and went to bed.

I was out of the door at six-thirty minus the scrambled egg because room service, which had been so incredibly helpful the night before, said they weren't open; I must have been misinformed, they claimed; they couldn't cook. So I had a banana sent up and in the meantime I drank two litres of water.

I walked across the road to South Kensington station and the first thing I saw was two other people with their marathon bags over their shoulders, and we went down to the platform where there were fifteen others, and that was when I started to feel really excited, that this was a big thing. And by the time we got to the Embankment, everyone on the train was a marathon person.

The special train from Charing Cross was where the party atmosphere started. There was a man wearing a wolf's outfit walking up and down the carriages and standing behind people just close enough to spook them. There was an Irishman who was sharing his stories with a friend and everybody in the carriage was listening. I was just kind of eyeing everybody up. It was fairly clear from what people wore, their bodies and general demeanour, whether they were at the faster end or the slower. It was just terribly exciting and felt really momentous.

When I got to Blackheath I walked the opposite way to everybody, to go up to the house of a friend who was running too. I was really glad because my levels of excitement and nerves were building up to where I felt I was going to explode. 'This is unbelievable! This is incredible! This is a key moment!' It was nice coming to my friend's house because it was very calm in there and I could talk to people about how I felt.

Until then I hadn't talked to anybody. I hadn't said a word till I walked into that house. I wouldn't recommend that to anyone, spending a marathon morning completely by them-selves. I was so undecided about what time I was going to run. I knew I wanted to try and do it in 4.30, but I'd had such a terrible half-marathon in March that I vacillated. Should I go for five? What should I do? What should I try? My friend's son was also running, and he said to me, 'Run with the pack until you get halfway. You'll think you're running too slowly, but don't try and get ahead of them. At halfway, assess the situation and if you think you can go faster then go ahead.' And it was really good advice.

I positioned myself near the *Runner's World* sub-4.30 pacers. I never heard the starter gun go off. I just heard a cheer, so then we all cheered. Before I even got to the start line I'd lost the pacers, so that was the end of that. But when we started shuffling forward, I was going, 'Thank goodness, thank goodness, it's beginning.'

It took sixteen minutes before I crossed the start line; I looked at my watch. When I crossed it, I thought, 'Ooh, this is exciting,' but immediately after that it was, 'Oh, what's the time? Down to work now.'

I thought it was so nice that so many people had decorated their gardens with flags and were sitting outside. A lot of them were drinking already, and it was barely ten o'clock in the morning. I thought, 'They're going to have problems later.' I felt very proud to be part of it. What felt weird was that this was one of the world's big races and we were running down these ordinary little suburban streets. I just thought, 'How strange this is.'

I did feel quite a lot of detachment at the beginning. I also felt the effect of drinking those two litres of water. I'd had one wee at the hotel, one at Charing Cross and one in someone's garden at Blackheath before I got to my friend's house, then two at my friend's house and one just before the start. An awful lot of weeing. And even then I did about 3 or 4 miles and needed another loo stop.

I was very lucky; I saw a Toilet sign on the high street. Someone just before me ran off and I just ran after him and into the toilet: no queue, I peed and ran out again. One minute. I ran another two miles and I thought, 'No, I still need another one.' There was a whole row of men lined up. I was so jealous of them. I saw steps leading down to a footpath and ran down there, thought, 'Sod it,' and pulled my knickers down. Three women followed me and I said, 'Sorry about my bare arse,' but they just squatted down beside me. So there we were, a line of bare bums. Well, it's only fair, all the men were doing it.

And then I just settled in. Not head down – I was really taking in everything on display. So many things to see. Things that made me laugh. Interplay between runners and the crowd. It was a really pleasurable few hours. A lot of the time I stood outside myself and thought, 'Wow! The London Marathon!'

I drank every Liquid Power drink that was available, carrying it with me and sipping slowly. Water at every stop. Five sips and then I threw it away. It felt terribly wasteful, but I didn't want to be carrying a bottle. It felt really good not to have anything in my hands.

But every 45 seconds – I was counting – I had a dull ache in my kidneys which I think was because I'd over-hydrated. I thought I had kidney damage! I was quite focused on whether the ache was going or not. It lasted for 7 or 8 miles and then it just went.

I saw two of my daughters, Sarah and Kathleen. I ran past; they were a few yards away and I shouted but they didn't see me. I saw David, my husband, and my other two children, Natty and Luka, at 11 miles. I liked seeing the landmarks too because I could count them down: 'OK, that's one gone – three to go.'

I'd already had a couple of moments when I thought I was going to cry because it was just so incredible to be part of it, but at Tower Bridge it all came over me. It was just one of the most fantastic moments of my life. The sun was shining brilliantly, reflecting on the water; the water was this aqua-green colour, all lit up. The bridge was crammed with people, and I did think about my dad then. The tears started to run but I thought, 'I don't want to be crying.' I felt really relieved to know I'd crossed the river.

I found running round the Docklands was the hardest part. You run past Canary Wharf and at every twist and turn you know you've got to get back to it, and it seemed interminable at that point. I got quite grumpy. I was composing this letter to the London Marathon organisers. 'Everyone who stops to walk must go to the side. There's got to be a *rule*.'

I saw a couple of people from the *Telegraph* team so we checked in with one another but I didn't really want to talk too much because I didn't want to waste energy. There were children running across the road; it seemed to be a bit of a sport and I found that *really irritating*.

The Docklands is where you see the people ahead of you for the first time, and I just wished I could go over the barrier and run with them. I'm glad I couldn't remember how many miles I had to go, though, because it was hard, it was a hot day. But I got round that bit, and the Tower of London, that's where I really, really started to feel on top of the world.

I didn't hit the wall at any point. I never felt like jelly. I had more of a mental problem than physical with Canary Wharf – all that winding round and back on yourself – but at the Tower of London I moved into feeling like I was hardly touching the ground from the cobbles onward. I felt really elated.

I knew I was going faster though I'd stopped timing myself. I'd been keeping to approximately 10-minute miles but I was ahead of myself on time, ahead of what I'd hoped to achieve. I didn't look at my watch again. My whole body felt lighter, my head felt lighter, it was ecstasy. I had been grinning a lot anyway but I was like the Cheshire Cat from that point onwards.

Running along the Embankment was absolutely unbelievable. There was a great steel band at the beginning of the underpass. I came out and I'd just seen my sister Charlie and her kids and I had a momentary flicker of tiredness and at that point I ran past a guy who was one-legged and on crutches and I thought, 'How can I be tired?' I was so full of admiration for him.

Finally I reached the Houses of Parliament. That was just very exciting. I crossed the finish line and I felt, 'I can go on, I can go on, I can go on running . . .' I slowed down to get my medal and that was when I got really choked up. They put one on the guy next to me and he just collapsed on the ground, sobbing.

I felt . . . surprised. Surprisingly normal. This is going to sound hideously cocky, but it wasn't as hellish as I'd expected it to be. I expected to be dragging my feet the last few miles. I certainly didn't expect to be standing there waiting for the bag with my clothes in, feeling as though I'd just done a training run.

I found a letter from Natty in my bag after the marathon. 'Dear Mum, I love you and I am so proud of you.' And that's when I thought, 'Maybe all those huge targets aren't as far away as they seem – climbing Everest, parachuting out of aeroplanes, things which seem to be far beyond a normal person's capabilities.' It made me realise there's no such thing as a normal person's capabilities.

I don't think I'll ever have a 100 per cent healthy attitude towards my body, but I'm 90 per cent more healthy about it than I was when I started. I thought when I started training that I'd be as fit as I wanted to be and the shape I wanted to be, and I now know that will never happen, but I've accepted that. I look at myself and think, 'Yeah, face is OK but the nose is too big. *Got* to get rid of the cellulite. I don't have a waist.' But I'm doing less of the looking at my body negatively. More than being obsessive about whether my thighs are the right measurement, I *feel* fit and healthy now and that's more important than a body which looks right in clothes. If your body's healthy, you're ahead, aren't you?

I did think about my father sometimes when I went out training. What to say? I wanted very much for him to be proud of me, and I was quite jealous as a child of the time and attention that he gave to the people who were his fans. And so I was quite needy of his love and approval, and it was something that I spent quite a lot of time talking about and getting clear in my head as an adult. It was resolved with him before he died, and though it's not the whole reason I did it, there was certainly a bit of me that was doing the marathon so that he could be proud of me.

To everyone who sponsored me:

Thank you! (a huge thank you) for your incredible generosity and support.

Together we raised £8,228.60 for the British Brain and Spine Foundation.

I completed the London Marathon in 4 hours and 25 minutes (including two loo stops!). All in all a magical day. THANKS AGAIN.

Caroline Taraskevics's marathon tip
If you're following a programme like the one supplied by the London Marathon, don't exceed it. The injuries I got were all a result of pushing myself harder than I needed to.

Steve Wehrle

Steve was coming back to London for the sixteenth year. He'd never missed one yet. Over the years he'd achieved some impressive times, but looking back he'd been younger then, hungrier, less preoccupied with work. He'd started off hoping for a sub-3.30 finish, but it was getting harder to put in the training miles.

At the beginning of February he'd put in a 57-mile week which included an 18-mile run on the Sunday. Then he did the Essex 20 on the 14th. He'd gone out ambitiously and felt good, he thought he was going to run a decent time. He'd done the first 5 miles in 35.40, the next 5 in 36 and the next in 37. Pretty reasonable. Then he got to just over 15 miles and started to fall apart.

The race was part of the Essex Championships but if he was being honest, it was fairly low-key. Not many there. And he'd always found it difficult to run four-lap courses, coming back to the same place every time. He didn't know if it was boredom or what, but he'd much rather have been running two 10-mile laps, or one 20.

He was racing against himself, and against a couple of other Dulwich guys as well. He was in front for 10 miles but they caught up and went on from him.

Realistically, he might have gone off too fast. Or maybe he hadn't done enough long runs before the race and because he was pushing it hard he'd started to suffer. But it wasn't a complete disaster. A 2.33 finish, that wasn't too bad.

The first weekend in March, he'd done a half-marathon, the Fourbanks, at a club down in Beckenham. Another multi-lap course. He'd run it OK, but it was down on what he could do. So two weeks later he'd gone off to do the Hillingdon Half-Marathon, thinking, 'Right, I've rested properly.' But he'd done virtually the same time, 98 minutes. Which was OK, but he'd hoped to get nearer 90.

The following week was his club's Richmond long run.

That was the one they used as a guide to London; it was 24 miles, cross-country. He'd always been able to calculate a London time based on what he did in Richmond. The year he'd run 2.59, he'd run Richmond in 2.44. This year it had taken him 3.15, so he was hoping from that to do London in 3.00 to 3.30.

Steve Wehrle's marathon

I have to say I never really recovered from the Richmond Long Run. I don't know why. I don't think I pushed it too hard. But there were two other guys who felt similar and neither of them ran London as well as they had hoped.

You could argue that you shouldn't do a 24-mile run that close to London, but I've done others the same and it's been absolutely fine. So I don't know what it was really. You can calculate from what you've done how you'll do in a 10k, a half, a 20, but a marathon's different. There's guys who've done all right and had awful marathons, and some who've done nothing right and had brilliant races. I've had 26 marathons now and I've only really been happy with four of them.

In the last week before London I did very little: 5 miles on the Monday, 6 on the Wednesday with the club and that was it till the Sunday. I did all the things you're supposed to do. Early nights. No booze. Good food. Plenty of water. Carbohydrate drinks. I drink banana-flavoured Leppin. I've used it for the last ten years or so. Whether it's psychological I don't know but it has worked for me in the past. But it didn't this year.

I did 3.55. Which was 26 minutes down on what I hoped to do. I was a minute a mile slower than I'd hoped. I was out on Blue Start for the first time in years. To be honest, I thought it was more difficult than Red Start. It was three minutes before we got moving.

I ran with a friend from the BBC for seventeen miles. We

were going fine; we were sort of on target for 3.30; we got to halfway in 1.44. But at 17 miles. . . . It's the wall thing, isn't it? I said to Roger, 'You go on, I'm beginning to suffer a bit.'

I never walk. I refuse to walk. I'm frightened to death that if I start walking I'd never run again. I kept going and a mile later I caught Roger up and passed him. Same thing had happened to him.

In the last 5 miles I was down to 11-minute miling. It took me 62 minutes to do the last 10k. There is no short cut. In 1991, I was doing 60, 70 miles a week. You've got to average 55 miles a week to run a decent marathon. This year I was doing 42, which is going to get you round but you're going to suffer in the later stages.

I found it in some ways one of the most difficult marathons I'd run because, ten years ago, I was running it an hour faster than I am now. I accept it. The worst thing people can do is not accept it. They get frustrated, but it's no good dreaming about what you could do when you were 40.

The one thing I did differently this year was that normally I cut back mileage quite dramatically in the last two weeks, but this year, because I hadn't done enough, I did 50 miles in the penultimate week and then cut right back. But we're all built differently.

I know I'm not training as hard as I used to. Quality and quantity not as much. The incentive doesn't seem to be there quite so much. It's hard to keep being hungry. And when you're running well you have the incentive and the confidence, but when you have a couple of races that don't work out, that's difficult.

I was disappointed, but not for any length of time. Once we got to the evening, I was thinking, 'What the hell. Another medal. Another year.' But I reckon it took me five or six weeks to get over it, physically more than anything. The year I ran 2.59 was the easiest marathon I'd ever run; I was over it in five days. I felt I was flying. It's the confidence thing, it's psychological. This year, I felt absolutely shattered, and when I did try to run there was no bounce, no spring, I was just plodding along. Worn out.

I'm going to do next year's, that's for sure. Under 3.30 is my prediction. After that, we'll see.

Steve Wehrle's marathon tip
The biggest mistake anyone can make is to go off too fast. You're really going to suffer later on.

Sophie Mirman

Sophie was running her first marathon; it was a challenge from her three young children. She hadn't taken part in any sporting activity since her schooldays, and after beginning her training from a very low base of fitness she was increasingly worried about her ability to get round. All through February and March she trained with her friend Polly. She hated it, but she kept going because she was raising funds for the Starlight Foundation.

She and Polly ran the Reading Half-Marathon. It was awful, the first warm day she'd been running. Polly would definitely have done a faster time had they not been together. Not a very pretty route, either. It was quite hilly and the last three miles were particularly ugly, through an industrial estate. Not a good motivation.

Because she'd had to give an estimate of her race time, she was right at the back with people who were in costume and there to have fun. She found it quite depressing, seeing people overtake her who were much older or who didn't look particularly fit. Two chaps who started with her and Polly were running it as a three-legged race: red wig, yellow wig, buckets to collect money. They finished in front of her. Sophie's children were so worried about how long she was taking that they came running back along the course to find her. It was quite demoralising. But her aim was always to get round the course without injury and in one piece, and that she did.

Three weeks before the race, she was so anxious that she was thinking of writing to people and saying she hadn't completed the course and would they like their money back. She had injured her back after her daughter jumped into her arms and she tried to lift her, so she had lots of massages for that. Then, as the marathon got nearer, everything seized up. She couldn't get her muscles loose again.

She was anxious because she was out of her territory. She was a businesswoman, not a runner. But she had to complete it. It was a challenge. She knew if she didn't complete it she'd have to do it again.

Sophie Mirman's marathon

The night before the race, I didn't sleep. The whole household was up at five-thirty. My mother had come over from France; it was her birthday. Richard, my husband, took the children off with her, and Polly and I set out.

We got to Charing Cross station. I've never seen so many runners, the place was completely packed with them. The train was very smelly. People were pushing and shoving. A man sitting opposite us had done three marathons. 'It was a doddle,' he said. 'Anyone can do it,' he said. 'Only 600 don't finish,' he said, and the more he said that the more I knew I was going to be one of the 600.

I was wearing a long-sleeved T-shirt and another T-shirt over the top because I always get cold; I don't get hot when I run. Because there was so much going on at Greenwich, Polly and I didn't actually hear the starter gun go off. We were still putting our baggage in the truck when we saw people moving forward. But we were right at the back. Time wasn't an issue. We could just pop in. As soon as we got through the gates we kept seeing people disappear behind the bushes. We thought it was a short cut they were taking but they were going for a pee. Women as well as men. At the start!

The first half was absolutely fine because Stephen, Polly's husband, had arranged to meet us at the 7-mile mark and then the 10. So instead of having to think of it as the whole 26 miles you had the easier target of knowing you could stop and have a drink and a little chat and then he'd pop up again further on. What did affect us was that we were psyched up to get our Liquid Power drinks and at mile 5 everything had run out – and at every station after that. There were people picking up half-drunk pouches from the road but I didn't fancy that. And because so much had been spilt, the soles of our shoes were sticking to the road.

We ran alongside two rhinos, James and Dan. My cousin had come over from Paris and at Tower Bridge we stopped and chatted. Up to then it was quite enjoyable. The weather was decent, we didn't have to go through any rain and cold, and at the halfway mark it was 'Yess! We're almost there.' And then came the downer. Then you saw thousands of people coming in the opposite direction.

It's fine if you're in those thousands but if you're stuck at the back it's demoralising. And it's the worst part of the route. There's nothing to look at, except the sign the other side of the barrier saying 22 miles. Your heart sinks. All these people coming towards you who've virtually finished the race. So near and yet so far. So tempting to leap over.

So 13 to 19 were horrible. I just didn't like it; my feet were hurting, my back was hurting. We walked a mile, ran a mile, and every so often we stopped to stretch. At mile 17 Stephen popped up with his mobile and I spoke to Richard on it, and he scooped the family up and took them to the finish. At mile 19 we reached the Starlight meeting point and had a huge cheer, which put us back on track, and after that it was fine.

We didn't hit the wall because we were going so slowly. It disappeared in front of us. We were behind a woman who was irritated that the crowd weren't cheering. 'Come on, give us a cheer!' she kept shouting and by the time they cheered she had moved on, so we got it instead. I thought the crowd were great. They encouraged me to keep on.

At 20 miles, we knew we were going to finish, and for the first time I felt confident. There was great excitement when you swept past Buckingham Palace; that was wonderful. You went through the finish line and there was a chap there with a tray of white bread, cheese and tomato sandwiches, and it was the best sandwich I'd ever tasted. It was absolutely delicious. I devoured it, and I'd never normally buy a white bread sandwich.

We just felt a great sense of elation. We'd done it. There's no question that Polly would have run it much faster than me but we stuck together through thick and thin. Her downs didn't coincide with my downs so we were able to pull each other through. For me it was a real personal challenge and I just felt absolutely delighted I'd done it because now I'll never have to do it again which is wonderful.

I think I've always been fairly determined. Once I'd decided to do it, I had to do it and there was no way I'd pull out. It was more of a physical challenge than anything else. I was so unfit when I started, I'd done nothing for years and I started from such a low base of fitness. I was really convinced that I couldn't do it and the main problem was getting over that. Now I think that if I can do it, anybody can.

I don't want to lose that fitness. The main thing I have taken away from the marathon is that as long as I don't have any injuries I will always run because I feel so much better for it. I go out three or four times a week but I'm enjoying it now; there's not the pressure of doing it for an aim. I do a short run, for an hour, and interestingly I've got fitter and faster since the marathon. I do 6 miles an hour rather than 5.

The next day I felt slightly stiff but absolutely fine. I had a massage and Polly and I went out and had a celebratory lunch at the Putney Bridge Restaurant. We walked there and had a couple of glasses of champagne and a very nice meal.

We promised you we would let you know just how Mum did in the London Marathon, how much we raised for Starlight and just how much you have helped the children you are supporting.

We are very proud to inform you that despite being overtaken by Beavis and Butthead, Superman, Batman (not Robin), three Clowns, four Rhinos and a Transvestite Nurse, Mum completed the Marathon and has raised over £12,000 in the process.

Oscar now has all the bones he wants, Dad has stopped cooking and life is generally returning to normal.

The Starlight Children's Foundation will now, thanks to you, be able to fund over 10 wishes which will help brighten the lives of seriously ill children at what can be the lowest point of their and their families' lives.

Thank you for your wonderful help,

Natasha, William and Victoria Ross.

Sophie Mirman's marathon tip
Make sure you have the right shoes.

Max Jones

Max never really had any burning ambition to run 100 marathons. There seemed little purpose in it when he had so many other priorities and there were enough nutters in the world without giving the impression – correctly – of being one himself. Then in 1998 he'd noticed that the total of his marathon and ultramarathon races was into the high nineties

– if you counted a 50k race as one marathon and, for instance, his M70 world record of 191k as just one also, not $4\frac{1}{4}$ marathons. So if he were to run the races he'd intended then London 99 would be his 100th. Then he missed a marathon because of an injury, so he needed another somewhere else for the 99th.

He went every spring and summer to spend a month in Portland, Oregon, with his daughter Amanda, who was a psychiatric nurse married to an American psychiatrist. They'd got three children. For several years he'd run in the Trail's End Marathon, which was on an out-and-back course. It started and finished in a little holiday town called Seaside. All the family would go there together. They'd get there on the Friday and on Saturday the children would play on the beach at Seaside while Poppa ran the marathon. Then they'd have supper in the Pig and Pancake after the prizegiving, and then they'd go 80 miles back home.

But this year there'd been three good reasons not to run it. One, it was on a new course. Two, it wasn't in Seaside. Three, it had been switched to May. So he'd had to look elsewhere for his 99th marathon. He chose the Napa Valley. He'd been invited to run it the year before but hadn't thought to book a hotel room in Calistoga, where the race started, until there weren't any left.

At the time he didn't run the 98 Napa Valley, he'd been staying with his friends Johnny and Ruth Anderson in Oakland. Ruth had invented Masters' running for women in the States 25 years back. She'd run over 100 actual marathons as well as over 70 ultras. But neither Max nor Ruth were morning people and they couldn't bring themselves to get up at four-thirty a.m. to make the seven o'clock start in Calistoga. That was why he hadn't run Napa Valley in 1998.

So in order to make sure of running it in 1999, Max and Ruth booked hotel rooms early this time, and on the Friday the two of them had a leisurely drive to Calistoga in Ruth's elderly Porsche. She was giving a talk at one of the seminars on the Saturday. She was also only going to run the second half of the course. Napa, she said, was a never-again marathon for her. Those dreadful cambers in the first ten minutes hurt her ankles so. The only time she did it, they were painful for weeks afterwards.

It wasn't immediately obvious to Max why the engineers had built the road that way, but he'd never seen anything like those cambers. But it was his 99th marathon; he had to finish in order to make London his 100th. So he went round all the many corners, as the road followed the line of the hillside, by running extra distance across them to get on the higher and generally flatter side of the highway. It was only the second race he'd ever run just to finish.

The other matter which concerned him, though not quite so seriously, was that he'd only been managing to average $15\frac{1}{4}$ miles a week in training over the last three months. Was his newly developed hypothesis of all-quality, no-junk miles going to turn out to be flawed in some unforeseen way? But he'd run a 96.45 half-marathon at the end of January – the equivalent of a 3.21.30 marathon – off the same training load, so off he set from Calistoga at 8-minute miling, 145 on his heart-rate monitor (without which he *did not race*!) looking for a 3.29 finish.

All went reasonably well until, er, $15\frac{1}{4}$ miles. There was a slight rise in the 16th mile and he found it a struggle. It took him 8.30. But then it was another 8.30 for the next mile, which was flat. After that he ran slower and slower to the finish. Over the last ten he averaged 9-minute miles. He finished in 3.41.45.

Even so, he was first M70 in what was the Road Running Club of America's Masters Marathon Championships. He was also less than seven minutes off the M70 course record.

The second M70 ran a 4.51, but the other three, in a field of only five, just beat the $5\frac{1}{2}$-hour cut-off. Yet another case of the competition thinning out in the higher reaches of the veteran running ranks.

He came down to London on Thursday 15 April. He wasn't up for it. He wasn't going for a time. He'd got himself injured on the Tuesday. A little thigh strain. The magazines said you should stop when that happens but if you did that every time you'd never finish a training session. So if it was a dull ache you carried on, if it was a sharp pain you eased off and if it came again, then you stopped and rang Maureen. It came twice in 50 metres so he walked home and got on the phone.

Maureen was the Valley Striders physio. She was a powerful woman. She was fit, was Maureen. Ten to fifteen years ago she was a silver medallist in the European Judo Championships, at one of the heavier weights – he didn't know which one because he'd never liked to ask. They were all frightened of Maureen because she made them scream. Or cry. What was worse, she had this treatment room with a curtain down the middle so you knew there was someone the other side of the curtain enjoying your pain.

Over the years they'd been ticked off so many times by Maureen. Two years ago his friend George turned his ankle over and didn't go and see her for a month, at which Maureen said, 'There's nothing more I can do for you.' Permanent damage resulted. So it was best just to go home and ring Maureen.

She called it softening. It seemed like an hour but it must have been three minutes. Pummelling it with her thumbs. Maybe she just did it for pleasure, he couldn't say. Cor, it was awful. And they paid her to do it. But he rang up Maureen and sure enough it didn't hurt at all by the day of the marathon.

Max Jones's marathon

Every London for the last twelve, I've stayed with Peter and Katy, my son and daughter-in-law. They live in Chesham near my good friend Chris, who's a mile closer to the marathon than Peter and Katy so we always stop and collect him on the way. This year we also had four South Africans with us, met on the road to Pietermaritzburg during the 1998 Comrades Marathon. Two were staying with us and two with Chris. They were looking for enjoyment and a 4.30 finish together.

On the day of the marathon, it was the usual routine: wake up at five-fifteen, eat two Power Bars, remember to put my heart-rate monitor on, go to collect Chris. We were five minutes late arriving at Chris's, and his windscreen was iced up. I de-iced it, then he found he needed petrol. He was just about to go back into his house to get money but we were getting later and later and I said, 'Don't go, I've got money,' so all that cost me £20 and some de-icing fluid.

It has to go exactly to the minute, but this year it was ten past seven – ten minutes late – when we got to The Strand. But we parked down John Adam Street as usual and managed to catch the weather forecast, like we do every year.

I was starting at Green Start. Chris, not being elderly or as good, was at Blue. I had a look round Red Start. I hadn't seen it for eighteen years. It's a lot cleaner than it was. As for Green Start, in 1993, when I was 65, there were about 150 runners there all told. Now there are men over 60, women over 55, Football Challenge runners, a few Fast For Your Age vets exiled from Red-Start-Outside-The-Gates, and Steve Cram. About 1,500, so I wasn't on the front row next to Cram and two of my Valley Striders clubmates but 25 yards away, which I calculated was 10.07 seconds from the actual start line.

I was *not* racing, only running to finish. Only the third marathon I've ever run in just to finish; the first was my first

London; the second, the Napa Valley Marathon on 7 March. That was my 99th, and I had needed to finish that if London was to be my 100th.

It was going to be a bonus if I recorded less than 3.49.57, which I did in the first London Marathon and which was still my Personal Worst. I've only ever been slower than that on the five occasions when I've been running an ultra in which I've been looking to record more than 100 miles in 24 hours. In fact I was aiming for 3.28: 8-minute miles.

Since the LA Marathon ten years ago, I've always chatted to the person next to me at the start and if I get no response I'll always meet someone in the first few miles hoping to do a faster time than they did last year. I'll say, 'Hello, what are you hoping for today?' So there I was at Green Start, 25 yards from the line, when at nine-twenty I met Karen. I said, 'How come a person as young as you is on Green Start?'

'I'm fast for my age,' she said.

It was only her second marathon, having run 3.46 last year, and she was bothered because there were so many people milling about and she was in the wrong pen. '*Don't worry*,' said I. 'I'm running my 100th and I'm aiming for 3.29. Stay with me and I'll see you through.'

We got to the first mile marker in 7.59. She was obviously very impressed! She didn't know that it took us 10.07 seconds to get to the actual start line, so we were a little too fast. But the London course is downhill for the first $3\frac{1}{2}$ miles and there was a slight westerly blowing us on our way.

Miles 2, 3 and 4 were 7.35, 7.30 and 7.30 as near as I could calculate while running at the same time. No worry, because it was the steepest downhill part of the whole route. My heart rate was above the 145/150 target rate I'd set, though. For various reasons, I hadn't had my haemoglobin count checked for about six months and I was slightly concerned that it might be too much up and that my blood was flowing less like Vimto and more like tomato sauce. So I turned the monitor's bleeper off so as not to alarm her too.

Mile 5: 38.21 was a bit too quick for 5 miles. It was time to slow down a little. I reprimanded Karen for not drinking all the carbohydrate drink and at 10 miles I said, 'Drink it *all*!' and she did a lot better. We were running in the middle of the road to avoid bumping into early walkers and others who had set off too fast and it was Karen who was collecting my water bottle as well as her own so we didn't collide into each other. I told her to pour all that she didn't drink over her head. I've not drunk any water as such, apart from what's in the carbohydrate drink, in my last 30 marathons; instead I get instantaneous cooling by pouring it over me. The other way, it could take 40 minutes to get through my internal pipework before it arrived at my skin as sweat. But on this day it was a very cold shower I was giving myself.

We were still, more or less, on time. The clock just checked to 1.35 as we went through the 12-mile marker. Going up to Tower Bridge, Ken Bingley and Terry Kelly passed us. I'd met them on the way in other races. 'What are you doing back here?' said Ken.

'I'm going steady, thank you.' Which I was at the time. I wasn't that bothered because I wasn't racing (I told myself) but I couldn't recall either Ken or Terry finishing in front of me in any marathon except in London 97 when I'd had an Achilles injury for the preceding fortnight and it went again at 5 miles. The problem with being an Ever Present is that we have to finish to retain our Guaranteed Entry and status, so 1997 was the first I'd run since 1981 when I registered over ten minutes for the mile which includes the Tower's cobblestones.

Karen and I went through halfway in 1.44-something but, with the narrowing of the course at that point and a trio overtaking us and interplacing themselves between her and me, she drifted away when I decided not to push through the

195

three-man barrier and catch her. I never saw her again, and because the London results as printed in *The Times* are so useless, I couldn't find out afterwards how many of the dozens in front of me from 3.29 onwards whose initial was a K. was a female called Karen.

I can't read my watch without my glasses too well, but I knew I was slowing. The clock at mile 15 had been showing 1.59-something but at mile 16 it was 2.08, at 17 it was 2.16 and at 18 it was 2.25. Other runners were passing me regularly, albeit not in droves, but the last 6 miles are always the most difficult, not because of the alleged wall at 20 miles but because there's usually a headwind.

But I also knew, from my ultramarathon experience, that I could run 10-minute miles for another 28 miles, never mind just 8, so I worked out I should be at the finish in another hour and 20 minutes, which meant I had almost five minutes to spare from my previous worst. So I thought I was probably running about 9-minute miles. I had a good bit in hand and people weren't passing me as often as they had been earlier in the race.

I was going slower partly because I wasn't fit enough and partly because for a shuffler like me the worst bit of the road surface is the cobbles. But I chased a man in a West Ham strip up The Mall and got to the finish in 3.42.42. And I was second out of the 180 people running for Age Concern.

There was no special feeling. None at all. I wasn't up for it before. I wasn't up for it after. If there had ever been any excitement at all, it was in saying, 'And it's going to be my 100th.' But I went through the finish, got my bag of not-very-goodies and climbed over a barrier to where the Age Concern people were having a little reception. Coffee, massage and a kiss from Polly the PR.

I'd been chatting for about a quarter of an hour when Polly said, 'We're going to make you a little presentation.'

I said, 'Oh no, I haven't got to make a speech, have I?' But

I went up and they gave me a bottle of champagne and I must say the tears were rolling down, then.

Max Jones's marathon tip
If you're on Green Start and you're hoping to do a faster time than you did last year, look for Poppa. I'll see you through. No sweat.

Jill Demilew

Jill was running to raise funds for Whizz-Kidz in memory of her daughter Miriam, who'd suffered from brittle bone disease. She'd been training with her friends Jen, Ros and Sarah. They'd done the Canterbury 10 together. It had been a beautiful day, but she'd had the ambulance up her bum for the last few miles. She really resented that. Being out there, nothing left to give. Then they did the Tunbridge Wells Half-Marathon, which was a stupid race to choose because it had a killer hill. She did almost exactly $2\frac{1}{2}$ hours because she saw the clock and thought, 'I'll be buggered if I finish in over $2\frac{1}{2}$.'

The day of the marathon got nearer. Two years previously, Sarah had overcome breast cancer; now, shortly before the race, she discovered another lump. She had a week of tests, with more to follow after the marathon. The results she'd got back by the day of the race were fine and the breast care nurse said, 'There's no reason you shouldn't do it.' Ros and Jen, the faster of the four, were going to run together. But Jill, she was going to stay all the way with Sarah.

Jill Demilew's marathon
There was none of that emotional, teary stuff that normally I get from just going to the start or watching it on TV. Ros and I arrived at the start in overtrousers; I had a pair of very expensive woollen trousers that had gone on the thigh. Jen

was aghast that I was going to dump them: 'But you can't throw them away.' By the time we were walking up to the start I had decided to take my jumper off and dump it on the first person I knew, who turned out to be someone who used to teach me midwifery in 1978. Jen was still going on about it when we were crowded in our pens. And during the first mile.

It's so busy in a marathon, you're busy just seeing everybody. At Charlton Road where it dips I couldn't believe it, the men were already peeing. It's the only time I've ever had penis envy. I wished I had one I could keep in my pocket and use as a conduit. Just as we were going past Charlton Park School Sarah and I saw Jen and Ros coming out of the bushes looking very comfortable, so we said, 'Blow it, this is our patch,' shook hands and dived into the bushes.

At Woolwich, Sarah's cleaning lady was there with a good luck banner, and so were our cheerleaders: Dan, Ros's mum, and three husbands dressed as Where's Wally. We were fine then, but by 14 miles we were having it hard. Commercial Road was the worst, with this stream of fit humanity coming towards us on the other side having already done 21 miles. I work over there and I knew exactly how far it would be before we got there.

Sarah's homeopath had given her something for the wall and something for her aches: crystals which her husband Mike was looking after. Coming up Canary Wharf, we saw our blokes. And when Mike gave us the bag we just couldn't get these things out. I felt really low. The blokes got them out for us and we were lapping the stuff from their hands, like dogs. But while we were on the island I saw a little boy with brittle bone disease. It wasn't a Miriam substitute or anything, but he looked bored, and when I shouted he gave the most brilliant smile.

We'd lost Jen and Ros, who apparently hit the wall. The youngest of us, too. Jen said afterwards that she was evil at

18 miles. Ros accused Jen of getting very actressy, she'd run along touching people's hands: 'Thank you, darling, thank you for supporting me.'

What was killing us was that the Liquid Power stuff ran out. I'd trained with it; psychologically I wanted it. It bothered me in the head. I picked discarded packs of the stuff off the ground. I was scavenging. Sarah said she was finding it hard but I said, 'I'm not leaving you. We're going to come in together.'

On The Highway I met somebody from work outside Babe Ruth's and she gave us a big, family-size pack of Rowntree's Fruit Pastilles. Our saving grace. I fed Sarah and myself and we swigged it down with water for the last few miles and by the Blackfriars underpass we were overtaking people. I said, 'Sarah, this is like the transition stage of labour. OK, we won't get a baby at the end, but we'll get a medal.'

She said, 'I'm in a trance now.' But then she shouted, 'There's Big Ben!' She looked wonderful. Tired but stunning, with her earrings on, and just a peek of her Marks and Sparks specials. We came in singing a hymn. It was a moment of pure joy.

Whatever success is, for me it's about loving relationships, the joy and the pain, whatever life throws at us. And I don't mean this in a wishy-washy way, this is through fire. I felt exultant.

Jill Demilew's marathon tip
The marathon is like life, it's the unknown.

Joe Fell

For most of his adult life Joe had been an alcoholic. When he stopped drinking at 44 he took up running to give himself something to do. He reckoned alcoholics had obsessive tendencies, and he'd taken that obsessiveness into his running. The difference was that now he was doing something that made him feel alive instead of slowly killing him. Running made him feel great, and he was good at it. He'd won medals. This was going to be his sixth London Marathon. He'd recorded a PB of 3.06.20 in 1997. He still thought he might have a sub-three in him.

Halfway through training, he ran the Fleet Half-Marathon in 1.29, which was a personal best. And he beat Chris Vernon. He loved to win, Chris. They were the two best over-50s in Dulwich Runners – among the younger runners as well. He knew Chris's trick was to stay behind you till near the line, but Joe beat him by four minutes. The race was lovely, the last few miles, feeling the wind in his back. He'd usually come in with the fast women, but that day he passed them all.

After the Fleet, his goal was to get his weight down. He lost 8lbs in four weeks. It was going well. Then about a week before London, he got a bad knee. Christ, it came on him, this lump on his knee; he thought, 'This is it.' He had two days off. The lump was still there. He went to a physio. She told him to do some exercises and they were a pure waste of time, like throwing snowballs in a fire. So, the night before, he tied a bandage round his knee to stop the vibrations coming up from his ankle, and that was him ready for the London Marathon.

Joe Fell's marathon

I was in the Fast For Your Age tent on Green Start when I met this fella and he was a doctor. I told him about my injury and he says, 'You've got runner's knee. You have an imbalance in your muscles. Get a 2lb weight and lift it up and down with your foot 20 times every morning.'

So anyway, I did the first 5k very well; I always measure my first 5k. I did 20 minutes for the 3 miles and then in another

34 seconds I reached the 5k. I thought I was going too quick so I pulled back and we got to the 10k marker in 42.29, which was what I wanted.

The funny thing was, I knew when I started to run that I was going to have a good race. Not a great race, but I had my dancing feet, when they just kiss the ground and there's great movement there. Like when you're sitting down and you have a couple of beers and feel like dancing.

I had my last drink on 18 September 1989. My family were quite happy to know I was killing myself with drink for years because I was doing it out of Ireland. Very good at sweeping things under the carpet, my family. Go in there, you'd trip over because there were so many lumps under the carpet.

My father died three years ago. He had a heart attack. Cigarettes. There was nothing else wrong with him, he was as strong as a horse. I stayed with him for three weeks when he was dying. I was glad I was there but I felt no grief at all because I'd seen so much. Why is it that when someone close to me dies I tend to forget it very easily? Maybe I put a barrier up. In the old days, it was easier to get pissed, I suppose. Drown my sorrows. And the next day you do it again, and the next, and the next. But I emptied all the shit out of my body ten years ago. It was like coming out of Vietnam. It's hard to ask me to shed a tear for anybody now. But I love running.

The year I did 3.06.20, I felt so light and lovely it was like a dream. I tell you, if you do a good marathon you remember it for the rest of your life. That year I was fucking floating! I passed all of the club boys, six of the elite boys. That was the one marathon I'll remember. And the year I did 3.36 when I nearly died. I nearly bloody died. Sometimes you know you're going to have a good marathon at the 6-mile marker. But if you're feeling bad at 6 miles there's another 20 to go.

But you've got to go on because otherwise in the morning you've got to live with yourself when you wake up.

Around the 10k point I was running with a couple of other Dulwich Runners, young guys, but they were going too quick for me so I let them go on. You've got to run your own race; don't let anyone else run it for you because it'll get you in the end. Marathons are fatal for getting you, your feet can feel like they're running through glue.

I got to the 30k point in 2.13.58 and at about 15, 16 miles I happened to pass the young guys again. That's why older guys are better at long-distance running. Not so much testosterone. These young guys see a nice-looking girl in front of them, you can see them speed up past her, as fast as they can. Then round the next corner they're puffing and gasping. If there was a nice-looking girl at every corner in a race, a young guy'd keep on going till he collapsed. Older guys just don't see the girl.

I got to the 40k point in 3.01.13 and finished in 3.12.05. It wasn't a super, super time but it wasn't too bad. I had loads in my body but at 20 miles my knee swelled up pretty bad and I had to pull back down. I wanted to finish because Chris Vernon was behind me.

My last 10k was 47.14 so it was a pretty even run. I'd got held up 3.04 seconds at the start because they'd put the Football Challenge runners in front of us and at the finish I looked up at the clock and thought, 'Ah Jesus, I've gone over the twelve,' but I didn't mind. I felt brilliant. Christ, I felt brilliant. You don't do this except you like doing it. I had a lovely race.

I didn't get tired. I had no blisters for a change. I could have run another 10 miles. I walked down to the baggage van, got my bag, got to Charing Cross and got on a train which pulled straight out. The journey took 25 minutes. About an hour after I finished I was sitting at home and there were still the 4.00 and 4.10 runners coming in. The next day I went out running again.

That doctor fella I met at the start, I never saw him after that, but I tried his exercises and blow me, three days later the knee pain had gone. I'll probably see him next year, we all meet up at the same place.

Joe Fell's marathon tip
The marathon is 75 per cent mental. It's easy to get physically fit but you've got to get your head in shape.

Gail Nerurkar

Bruce Tulloh's rule of thumb was that if your five longest runs added up to 100 miles then you were 100 per cent prepared for the marathon. So Gail was hoping to do sufficient long runs to fulfil that, fitting them in round her work as an epidemiologist and GP. What was good was that she had the support of her husband Richard. He'd decided he wasn't fit enough to do himself justice in London. It was his living, after all. But it was kind of nice to have your supper prepared and your bath run by an international marathoner when you came in from training.

It was Gail's first marathon, and she'd been doing some quite hard stuff in the first week of February; really good running, but the result was that by the beginning of the second week she'd noticed her resting pulse was up to 51, and then 53 the next day. She actually responded to that, because why bother to measure it if she wasn't prepared to do something about it? Her body was trying to tell her something. So she took three days off.

Doing that was hard, because she'd been gaining confidence from getting the miles in. And she felt OK, that was the frustrating thing. But she figured the combination of running and the rest of what she'd been doing had got too much, and her body was saying, 'Hang on a bit – let me catch up.'

But the next week she did a long run on the Saturday with Richard and his brother Ian. That was a real highlight. She and Richard went up north to Sheffield where Ian lived with his family. They did 32k altogether. Ian was a similar standard to her and because Richard was just easing back into light training, their sort of pace was fine for him. It was pretty amazing, Gail found herself thinking, to be able to share that sort of thing with your brother-in-law. He was eighteen months older than Richard, a GP. He'd got really into running in the last two years. He'd joined a Sheffield club.

The last weekend of February, she did the Bramley 20. She had a time goal of 2.20 and just wanted to run an even pace. The reason she chose Bramley was that it also had a 10-miler and her sister Bridget, who was a violinist and took up running a year back, had asked her for a 10-mile training schedule for Christmas. Bridget ran a superb race, 83 minutes, and had a great time, and Gail did 2.19.57 and finished ninth. It was a good day for both the girls.

On 7 March she did her first three-hour run. She'd woken up thinking, 'Phew, today's the big one.' She'd arranged to run the middle hour of the three with her friend Rachel, and she started out just before seven in the morning with her little gel belt on. She'd fixed up to run with Rachel because that way she could really think of the run in three stages. An hour to fill on her own – easy. Then Rachel with her for the middle stage, which was brilliant, an hour and a quarter in fact; they just kept each other going. And after Gail dropped Rachel off at her house she knew she only had another 45 minutes to complete. She reckoned she'd run 38k. And then she applied the rule that if you ran for more than $2\frac{1}{2}$ hours you didn't have to go to morning service because you'd only fall asleep in the sermon. So she went to evening service instead.

The rest of training went well. She did notice, though, that as the big day approached she was getting really keyed up. She had the feeling that there was an enormous event coming up, a bit like a final exam.

Gail Nerurkar's marathon

You're going through it in your head. I'd run part of the course and in previous years I'd driven round the whole thing in the early morning behind Richard when he ran it in training. It's that sense that you don't really want to plan beyond it, you just want to concentrate on it.

I took Friday off work so I didn't have to come into contact with people with colds on the train. Training had gone really well. I practised with my drinks; I could tolerate Liquid Power. I really felt, given reasonable conditions and some company, that I could have a good run.

Bruce and Sue Tulloh came to stay two nights before the race. I went out for an early jog on Saturday morning, and just felt slightly queasy when I came back. I thought, 'Maybe this is just nerves.' I lay down on the sofa for a bit but then in the next hour or so I started having awful diarrhoea and profound nausea, a really horrible feeling, and terrible vomiting.

But I wasn't going to give up. Richard was doing commentary for the BBC and had gone to rehearse on the commentator's motorbike and I decided to go into the race hotel where we'd both been given a room. I was unable to eat or drink which was ironic, when I was meant to be carboloading.

I went straight to bed when I got there, still hoping that I'd be able to do it the next morning. I pinned the number on my top, I tied the Champion Chip on my shoe. In some ways it worked for me because I was so sick that I was too exhausted to be emotional. I had this sense of foreboding but I was still hoping, hoping, really. Richard was just trying to console me. I think he knew that it was very unlikely I was going to get over it.

Through the night I was still sick. The blackest hour was about three in the morning. I knew there was no way I could run the race.

So then real despondency set in. Richard had to get off on the motorbike at half past six. I was left in this heap of sheets feeling sick and weak and dizzy. But I wanted to watch. I turned on the TV. The worst moment was seeing the elite girls lining up and seeing one of my friends giving a hug to the girl next to her and that was when I cried. I was completely overwhelmed by tears and I was on my own. Richard was doing his commentary but he phoned me just after the women had started. I think he knew I'd feel pretty awful then.

It was, I suppose, a bit similar to my experience of not making the final cut for the lightweight boat when I was at Cambridge. Something major that you've been building towards for some time has been pulled from under your feet – but that was different in that I obviously wasn't good enough to be in the lightweight boat and there was a decision made by someone else that I was out. This was infinitely more arbitrary.

We dragged home. One of the first people I wanted to get in touch with was my running partner, Rachel, but when she answered the phone I was still so upset I could hardly speak to her. But through the evening, several other people phoned and I began to be able to talk about it and I'd say that by the end of Sunday evening I'd had a drink by then and some toast, and I was able to think about what I was going to do next. I suppose it was a coping mechanism.

So with Richard and Bruce's help I decided that if I'd recovered by Tuesday or Wednesday I'd try for a marathon on the following Sunday. There were four possibles: Shef-field, Fort William, Gosport and Stratford – which was what I decided on because it was the nearest and we could stay at my parents' house in Oxford the night before.

I couldn't get really excited, I couldn't get keyed up all over again. I just thought, 'I've gotta do it,' and so I did. I went. I ran. I enjoyed it. 3.13.

Gail Nerurkar's marathon tip
Watch the rice pudding before the race.

Antony Read

Since he lost his right leg below the knee after a hit-and-run accident in 1980, Antony had dreamed of being the first amputee to run the London Marathon. Chris Moon beat him to it by eighteen months but Antony was determined to finish ahead of Moon's time. By the time he was 18, he'd already run a 3.05 marathon. Even after the accident, he was a fit, strong guy. Doing this one in a sub-four time needn't be beyond him.

The build-up was full of ups and downs, though. Near the end of January, he did the Mitcham 25k and it was a dream run. He'd been hoping to average 8.40-minute miles so he started with the *Runner's World* 9-minute-mile guy. It felt a very relaxed pace. He'd aimed to take off after the first 5-mile lap and up it to 8.30-minute miles.

What had actually happened was that he'd missed the 5-mile marker altogether. So he'd clocked himself at 10 miles and realised he'd been running 7.45-minute miles. He thought his watch had gone wrong. He'd been using everyone else in front of him as staging posts: looked at them and slowly reeled them in.

That had been one of the things the Mitcham 25k taught him, one of the best things he'd done that day. Start steady and be the bugger who catches everyone up. A brilliant way to run. He enjoyed the thought of it, the image of people reacting as he came past them. Anyway, he'd been hoping for 2.25 and he ran 2.08.51.

He'd felt so big and right that day that he knew now he could run the marathon distance. But then had come the Big But. He'd been on a high, he'd had a good morning. He'd got home early and made the decision to take his son Stuart out on his motorbike. Antony took a bike out to go round on. The upshot was, he didn't get the rest and recovery in. Instead, he was lifting the trailer around, and then his back started to hurt and it got worse. That night he'd gone to bed feeling rather uncomfortable and on the Monday he'd woken up to find he'd strained his back and trapped a nerve in his leg. He couldn't get out of bed.

He couldn't believe what he'd done. He'd broken one of his golden rules – rest and take it easy after a long run. He had to take a complete week out of training. By the end of the week it was better but still not right. And the following week he'd done a 4-miler and two weeks after that he'd done a 15, which was two laps of Richmond Park with Whizz-Kidz. He suffered after that. Aching thighs. Unbelievable.

But the way he looked at it, that had been an early warning. He wasn't invincible. He'd always got to rest after a good, hard run. But it was starting to be a worry, that between then and the marathon his back would go again. He told himself he wasn't going to dig the garden, he wasn't going to do anything, he was just going to concentrate on training.

The end of that month, February, he ran the Brighton and Hove Half-Marathon and did 1.47.46. He'd worked his way through the field, ended up on a cliff top. He'd been overtaking people, and as usual realised some must have been thinking, 'I'm not going to be overtaken by *him*.' There'd been one guy, Antony would overtake him, then the guy would catch up and pass Antony and slow down, and Antony would overtake him again. Less than half a mile to go, the guy had caught him up at the top of this slope. Antony had known the guy was poised to come past so he'd said, 'Sorry,' and just *went*.

Looking back on the weeks leading up to London, Antony knew that he'd been through a heavy training load. When you'd been gone as long as he had, fifteen years, when you hadn't run the long distances before, it was like . . . hard to describe, but he'd been running towards home thinking, 'I can't *believe* I'm doing this.'

He knew he was going to have problems with his left foot. It had blistered at the Gatwick half-marathon and he'd also lost every single toenail. He'd never had black toenails before, never knew they happened. And though he couldn't have explained it, he still didn't feel like a long-distance runner.

Antony Read's marathon

I'd decided to go with the *Runner's World* sub-four pacers but we lost nearly thirteen minutes on Blackheath Start when they'd only figured on losing six or seven. The pacer had to up the pace and I thought, 'This is a bit of a tall order for me,' but I decided to go with it. We ran an 8.05 through the third mile and we were overtaking people by the hundred, jumping into gaps and up and down kerbs. I don't think anything prepares you for London. It's far worse than you expect. So many people around you, closer to you, than any other race. But at the time I thought nothing of it; it was like running down a crowded shopping mall.

It didn't really thin out till 6 or 7 miles had gone. From then I enjoyed it – well, I enjoyed it all mostly, but from 7 to 15 was the best, when the pack had thinned. Tower Bridge was phenomenal. I'd always imagined it would be. Normally in a race you don't notice the sights, but at Tower Bridge you can't fail to notice – the thick crowds pinned back by the metal railings and leaning over – the sight of that great big blue and white thing. There's just something special about it – you're crossing into the City of London, the centre, and there's no traffic that day, it's a totally different place, it's like somewhere else.

Then you go down the dual carriageway. It's a lot easier there. Every 100 yards at least, if you've got your name on your T-shirt somebody calls it, which is good. A lot of people don't notice my leg, it's the last thing you expect to see. A bloke alongside me said, 'You look as though you're enjoying yourself. You've done this before, haven't you?'

I was still going with the pacer, but following her was a heavy task on its own. We got to the 15-mile mark. She was on the other side of the road, starting to head away, and I thought, 'I'm not going to sustain this pace. She's trying to run a 3.45, let's back off and go for the unofficial sub-four.'

By 16 miles I'd dropped to 9-minute mile pace. Around Canary Wharf, going over the suspension bridge, up and down, that felt horrible; my leg. Somebody behind me said, 'I've been along this so many times and I always forget how bad it is.' I'm starting to feel it a little bit but I'm basically OK. Then I got to 18-ish and it happened. The muscles on the inside of my thighs suddenly went and I've never had a problem with those muscles before. I didn't realise at the time but later I worked out it had been caused by all that dodging left and right and up and down in the first 6 miles, which under normal circumstances you never do while running.

I looked at my watch and I thought, 'I've got an hour and a quarter to do the last 8 miles in and what have I done wrong?' I'd been confident of getting to 21 or 22 without any problems, but now at 18 miles I had muscles hurting that had never hurt before. Psychologically, that was a low point.

So I dropped the pace again. The thought of not finishing didn't really enter my mind; I was going to finish at all costs. I was thinking I might still just make the four hours; you start doing sums in your head. I felt the blisters on my foot starting to go, which was a double blow, so it was, 'Let's just push on as well as we can and get ourselves up to the 22-mile mark.'

The muscles hurt but they didn't get any worse. You find yourself starting to count the miles down – the next mile marker, the next drink station. At 20 miles I grabbed bottles of water and decided to walk a little bit while I was drinking. I was drinking the whole bottle by then. I think my body was trying to tell me something. I just started drinking and couldn't stop.

The cobbles were terrible. Worse than I expected. Great big lumps of rock. Really threw me about. But I got to the 22-mile marker and thought, 'OK, I've gone through 4 miles like this, I can get through the other 4.' The four-hour target was starting to slip but at that point it was just 'go on and do the best you can'. Looking back, I think I was quite wise on the day. When I hit problems, what I did was the right thing every time.

I finished in 4.25 and I felt absolutely shattered. I've never been so shattered in all my life. And I was starving, and I've never been starving after a run, either. I didn't feel any elation. I always thought it was going to be very emotional but I was just so pleased to be able to stop running. I've got one big regret. I wish I'd turned round and looked back at the palace and everyone coming in behind me.

There's nobody there to greet you or anything. Only runners who feel the same as you. It's a very quiet and personal moment. The first railing I came to, I leant on that for a while. I went from railing to railing until I found a drink. I walked slowly, and got my goody bag and found a chocolate bar. I'd spent all my energy. All I wanted to do was sit down. So I plonked myself against the scaffold tower and started eating, and someone came and sat beside me. And then I got my kitbag and phoned up on my mobile and spoke to my mate who was waiting up by Admiralty Arch. I said, 'That's a long way from here,' and he said, 'What d'you mean, it's a long way? I can see the finish from here.'

And then I just slowly walked up to the arch, promising myself that I'd never forget how shattered I felt, and that when I do it again I'll make sure I won't feel the same way.

Antony Read's marathon tip
Believe me, with today's technology distance running isn't difficult for amputees and I hope as a result of my achievement others will be encouraged to take it up, because competing in road races with able-bodied runners is a very satisfying feeling.

Jessamy Calkin

When she'd started training she'd known that, left to her own devices, she wouldn't have stuck to it, so she'd asked Jo, a colleague, to help. Jo was a features assistant on the *Telegraph* magazine. There were several people in the office who ran but Jo really loved it and Jessamy knew she would see her as a challenge. And Jessamy didn't know her very well, which she liked the idea of. Because it was a whole new side of things.

Jo was Australian. She was very athletic. Jessamy got the impression her whole life was training. She cycled every-where. On her holiday she'd gone off and climbed Kiliman-jaro. She did kick-boxing. She did triathlon. The two women had nothing in common at all.

Jo wrote out a schedule for her to follow. Because no one at work knew what Jessamy was doing, it felt like she and Jo were having an affair. They'd sneak off together. Jo went to the gym ahead of her. Then Jessamy would follow. Jessamy quickly found out everything about her, because Jo would have to talk to her non-stop for self-preservation. If she didn't keep talking then Jessamy would start abusing her for making her do all these things.

There were still so many people Jessamy hadn't told about the marathon. People who she'd actually tell about even quite minor things. She didn't like talking about it in the same way that she didn't like people discussing diets. She wanted it to be like a job. Finish running and go home. If there was any consolation to be had at all from this terrible project, it was the idea of going into the office on Monday 19 April having run a marathon and no one knowing.

She disliked it so much. It was like having a really awful job that you did at night but you had to do it. It felt so out of character. At the office, if someone said to her, 'Did I see you running at lunchtime?' she'd always lie about it.

She'd been expecting all that to change. Her friends tried their hardest to convert her. They'd say things like, 'You'll hate it at first, but after a while you'll love it.' Or, 'You'll lose masses of weight.' Or, 'You'll go through this intense psychological thing.' It hadn't happened. For a start, she hadn't lost any weight. She was eating twice as much.

It was her first experience of doing something she loathed and not walking out. Jo kept saying, 'You're doing really well! Fantastic!' And it meant absolutely nothing to her. She was running the marathon because she didn't want to. If she didn't make it, she wouldn't feel like she'd failed. She didn't feel proud of it. For instance, there was the time she and Jo went out to buy gymbags. Jo found herself a very sporty one. Jessamy chose the least sporty of all, something that might look as if she was going away for the weekend.

She deliberately didn't try to get sponsorship – that would have meant more pressure, more people to let down. All those starving children. She did offer to earn some money for her daughter Bam Bam's playgroup but the organisers said, 'Don't bother, we're going to close down anyway.'

And the weather had been awful. Cold, wet and windy.

She didn't like physical discomfort of any kind. She thought it would be boring to start with, but get better. Instead she found it got progressively more uncomfortable. The little, short runs she and Jo had been doing at lunchtime hadn't got any easier. She'd had a terrible sore throat for three days: temperature of 102, headache. She'd given in and started taking antibiotics. She hadn't been in to work. She was feeling more and more pessimistic because she felt so awful physically. She'd ached for three days after her last 7-miler. She hadn't done a run that long on concrete before.

She was dreading it. She was going to work out exactly what she was capable of, because she had to have a little goal, and after that she could stop and walk. She knew it was going to be ghastly and she couldn't wait till it was out of the way. It was the blight on her horizon. It reminded her of when she was at school, with exams coming up.

She still despised runners. Perhaps not as much as she used to, but she still couldn't believe she was one of them. They'd got an expression of smugness about them even when they were wet and cold which she'd never seen on anyone else and which she couldn't bear. There was a guy in her office who ran and went to the gym, who was so narcissistic, so obsessed with his body she wanted to slap him.

Where running was concerned, with a certain amount of training anyone could do it. Whereas when you wrote an article, only you could do it in a particular way. With running, there was no creative expression. She'd never had any particularly interesting thoughts while doing it. She hated the way it made you sweaty and uncomfortable. She hated the clothes. They were all so hideous. Normally, she'd never have worn trainers because she couldn't bear them. She hated the trainer culture. People said that running made you free, but it didn't do that for her. Her idea of freedom was being in her car.

Around nine o'clock on the evening before the marathon, I got a phone call from Jessamy's friend Rachel. 'I don't know how to tell you this,' she said. 'Jessamy's lost her trainers. She might not be able to do it.'

'I've got plenty of spare trainers she can choose from,' I said. 'Tell her she can't get out of it. There is no hope. She is going to have to run the London Marathon.'

Jessamy Calkin's marathon

The longest run I did was the Sunday before the marathon, with Jo's boyfriend. Four laps of Clapham Common (10 miles) and walked home (3 miles). Jo thought that if I ran with him that, as I didn't know him, I wouldn't be able to abuse him too much. It was tedious but not too vile. We talked about how awful Jo is. He told me about previous marathons he'd run with her. He absolutely worships her so I knew he didn't mean it.

And then I didn't do anything except go into the gym one lunchtime to have a fitness assessment. I was a bit fitter. Very good aerobic capacity but everything else not very good. There were lots of *Telegraph* marathon runners going through their stretches and desperate to get on the machines.

We went to Run and Become as well because Jo said I had to have shorts. She'd ordered all this stuff. Power Bars, Squeezy, this foul drink which she made me have. She made me try on everything I was going to run in. The shop assistant said to me, 'What's the matter?'

I said, 'I can't believe I agreed to do this and go out in public looking like this.'

She said, 'What are you worried about? Lots of people have to run the marathon in fancy dress.'

'This *is* fancy dress,' I said.

All that last week, there were so many surreptitious conversations, notes sent to each other: how did I plan to carry the

Squeezy stuff? When was I going to drink the drink? Little packages to and fro. It was like being on drugs. On Friday someone asked me, 'What are you doing this weekend?'

'Running a marathon,' I said.

He laughed, thinking I was joking.

I must admit that, when I first started training, I was planning on pretending that my back hurt and that my doctor said I couldn't do it, but as time went on I realised, 'I can't pretend. I can't do that.' Jo was really excited about it. The contrast between her attitude and mine: so different. And it was highlighted by when we went to register.

Jo: 'Let's go now. Let's go early.'

Me: 'Why?'

When we got to the London Arena, her eyes lit up. She got really animated, like she was in Harrod's sale or something. I thought, 'I'm in hell.' I felt I was surrounded by people of a different species. They were all shapes and sizes and nationalities, but it was like going to a country where everyone else speaks French or Israeli or something, and you don't. Everyone knew something and I didn't.

I couldn't have got as far as I did without her, because she was really tough on me. The more she got to know me, the tougher she was. She started to know my little ways of getting out of things. She was very patient about my complaints. But the day before the marathon, I felt really tired all day. I thought, 'Maybe I'm pregnant. I can't run a marathon if I'm pregnant, can I?' Because when I was pregnant with Bam Bam that was the first symptom: being really exhausted. And if it had just been down to Jo, I could have got out of it, because she said, 'Oh, if you're pregnant you can't do it.' But then I made the mistake of telling my friend Rachel. She said, 'Of course you can do it. It'll love it, won't it? Great exercise.'

About eight o'clock on the night before the marathon, Jo came round. We were going to go to Rachel's, because

Rachel was going to walk the last two hours with me and we had to arrange where to meet. Jo said I was behaving like a toddler: the way I kept saying, 'Oh, do I have to?' She was refusing to let me take my radio to the marathon so I could listen to *The Archers*. She said, 'There's so much going on out there. I want you to absorb the atmosphere.'

She made me go upstairs and get all my stuff. I picked up my gymbag, emptied it and realised my trainers weren't in it.

Although I'm quite scatty, I've never done anything like that before. I do lose things a lot, but my trainers have always been in my gymbag. I felt gripped by panic. 'Jo!' I shouted. 'Something terrible's happened!'

'What? What?' Jo and Ralf, my partner, appeared at the bottom of the stairs.

'I've lost my trainers,' I wailed.

They came up and helped me look but I knew the trainers weren't in the bag, weren't in the house, and that when I'd had the gym assessment during the week I must have left them in the changing room. But now it was after eight o'clock on a Saturday night.

I didn't know the surnames of the people who ran the gym, so I rang Security at Canary Wharf and I got through to a very unintelligent-sounding guard who, when I asked him if he would go into the gym and look for my trainers, said, 'No.' I'd have to go in.

So then Jo rang him and persuaded him to go and have a look. She told him she'd ring him back in 20 minutes and in the meantime we drove to Rachel's with me thinking, 'How embarrassing will it be to say I can't do the marathon because I've lost my trainers?'

But when we got to Rachel's, Jo rang Security at Canary Wharf again and the guard said he'd found them. So then I knew there was no get-out.

At Rachel's I tried on all the gear. I thought I'd be on my

feet for seven hours, so I worked out I needed fourteen Squeezy things. I had them all round my waist on a Velcro belt and I felt like I was in a Western. We couldn't agree whether I was going to wear shorts or tights, or how many T-shirts I was going to need. Jo was cooking me pasta, which I don't like very much. I'd had no alcohol for a week, except on my birthday. I felt more and more despondent. I read the instructions the organisers had sent out: 'Make sure you're at the start well before 7.30.' I said, 'I'm not going to stand in a field for two hours.'

Jo: 'Oh, it's a lovely atmosphere, you'll love it!'

Me: 'For all of three or four minutes. What am I going to do for the rest of the time?'

I asked Ralf to collect my trainers from Canary Wharf for me, but he said, 'No,' because it's so hard to get into the *Telegraph*, you can't park outside. So I went, picked up the trainers and set straight off back. I was a bit worried. It was pretty late by then. I hadn't got anything ready.

Driving towards the Rotherhithe Tunnel, the car in front of me braked. I braked. The car behind me didn't brake. It was a pretty big whack. My glasses jumped off my nose; ashtrays flew out; everything fell off seats. The adjustable back of mine went into Recline. When I realised what had happened, I was almost lying down and I couldn't see anything because I didn't have my glasses on.

The guy who'd run into me, a real wideboy type, a middle-aged Del Boy, came running up to ask if I was all right and I said, 'Can you find my glasses?' I must have been in shock because then I got out and walked round to sit in the passenger seat. Another man appeared from nowhere. He was a doctor. He took my pulse. 'It's 100,' he said. 'Don't move.'

'I'm meant to be running the marathon tomorrow.'

'Well, you can forget about that.'

The ambulances came. The police came. It took ages

because they had to take down everyone's details. Del Boy came over and told me he'd been daydreaming and didn't see me. I said, 'I'm meant to be running the marathon tomorrow.'

He said, 'Oh, let me know if you do because my flat overlooks the route.'

Later I overheard him tell the police he'd braked, but skidded. He didn't have a tax disc. The police breathalysed him. They breathalysed me, which made me laugh. I said to the policewoman, 'You're welcome but I haven't been allowed to drink for a week. I'm running the marathon tomorrow.'

She said, 'I don't know what's wrong with you people.'

The guy who'd been in front of me went off in an ambulance but I felt OK apart from a headache. I was more worried about the car, the fact that it was making a terrible noise and that Del Boy had said, 'I just posted a cheque off to the insurance company today.'

When I got home, I refused a drink and ate a bowl of pasta in case I felt better by the morning but by the time I got to bed I'd sort of resigned myself to the knowledge that I wasn't going to do it. I was hoping I'd wake up after the marathon had started but of course I woke up at six. My neck really hurt. And I went and made myself a cup of tea and thought, 'Well . . .'

I felt a real sense of anticlimax. The car was outside, looking miserable. I rang Jo. I told her about my neck. She said, 'Hmm. So you won't be able to do it? Oh my God, you've got carboload, you'll have to go for a run anyway!'

So I went back to bed till the runners had definitely gone and then I lay in a lemon bubble bath listening to *The Archers* and feeling really grateful that I wasn't running in a line of people round Docklands. And when it was over I thought, 'Well, it's finished now and that's it.'

Jessamy Calkin's marathon tip
Go by car.

Endpiece

Joyce Chepchumba won the women's race in a desperate sprint after battling it out with four others from 18 miles. Chepchumba beat the world record for a women-only race. Her 2.23.22 netted her $230,000. Three of the others ran PBs. Manuela Machado set a new world veterans record.

Abdelkader El Mouaziz was first man home after bolting from the lead pack at 7 miles to chase down the pacemakers. He was the only runner inside 2.09. He was pursued to the line by Antonio Pinto, who tried to close the gap with one of the fastest final 5ks in marathon history. Abel Anton out-kicked Jon Brown on the way to third place and a 2.09.41 finish. Brown was fourth in 2.09.44. It was that close.

And so second by second, hour after hour, the rest of us came in. We charged, we sprinted, we limped, trudged or staggered. Two of us got married, stopping off at a church in Charlton two miles into the course to be spliced at top speed by a waiting vicar. Me, I did a PB for the first 10k, dropped back at 10 miles to run with the *Runner's World* sub-four pacer, found that too fast by 16, stopped for a *pause pipi* and lost the plot completely. Considered giving up, walked/ran, walked/walked, wept all the way down Narrow Street (wall stuff) and only got it back together in time to run round the corner into The Mall. Three minutes slower than my previous Personal Worst. It was that bad.

You go through it all in your head for weeks afterwards. That third weekend in March, when I'd attended the final day of my counselling course instead of running Brentford, was when I passed up my chance of doing a decent marathon. I know now that the thread which had bound me to my training had broken. The Sunday after Brentford, I only ran for an hour and by the time I got to Red Start in Greenwich Park I'd done too few long runs and not enough races. I'd had too many conflicting commitments. I'd just left the marathon emotionally.

But a couple of days later, I was pulling on my trainers and stepping out of my front door the same as I'd done in the aftermath of London for three years, and the same as I'll probably do until the only way I get out of my house is horizontally, feet first. I went easy across the heath and steady through the village. My legs were heavy but my heart, as ever, light. I thought of myself a year along the line, joining together with 30,000 others to run the first London Marathon of the twenty-first century . . . muttering about the time it took to get to the start line and still looking for a sub-four finish.

A special acknowledgement to Jane Cowmeadow and Sarah Blandford of the Flora London Marathon for all the help and information they so efficiently and good-naturedly provided.